PISTOL PETE MARAVICH
The Louisiana Purchase

PISTOL PETE MARAVICH
The Louisiana Purchase

by
Tom Saladino

THE STRODE PUBLISHERS
HUNTSVILLE, ALABAMA 35802

ACKNOWLEDGMENTS

I would like to thank all those people who helped make this book possible by supplying the material needed for such an undertaking: Pete Maravich; New Orleans owner Fred Rosenfeld; Jazz Public Relations Director Bud Johnson; Hal Hayes; former *Atlanta Constitution* staffer, Mike McKenzie, *Tuscaloosa News;* Bert Rosenthal, Associated Press; Bob Johnson of Atlanta; Bud Skinner of the *Atlanta Constitution*; Lewis Grizzard of the *Atlanta Journal*; Ed Baker of the Omni group; Paul Manassah of LSU; Nick Curran of the NBA; and the Atlanta Hawks publicity department.

Copyright 1974
By Tom Saladino
All Rights In This Book
Reserved Including The Right
To Reproduce This Book Or Parts
Thereof In Any Form — Printed In U.S.A.
Library Of Congress Catalog Number 74-15507
Standard Book Number 87397-056-X

Contents

1. Pete Comes Home 9
2. New Orleans Side Of The Trade 14
3. Before The Trade 21
4. Suspension 28
5. It's A New Ballgame 33
6. Pete, The Improviser 45
7. A Rembrandt 52
8. Looking Back 61
9. Pete's Second Year, 1971-72 74
10. Pete Signs With The Hawks 81
11. The Summer Of Waiting 88
12. Pete's Rookie Preseason 93

13.	The Long Season	98
14.	Pete's First Pro Game	105
15.	Superstar In The Making	108
16.	Pete's College Years	111
17.	Poppa Press And Scotty Robertson	120
18.	How To Do It Pete's Way	128
	Statistics	135

Foreword

Pete's accomplishments on the court are well-known and need not be recounted here. What impressed us was his overwhelming desire to play winning basketball and to help us build a winning franchise. He demonstrated this desire, in our opinion, by waiving the no-cut, no-trade aspects of his contract.

The decision to bring Pete Maravich to New Orleans was primarily a basketball decision as contrasted from a public relations or sales decision. We were aware of his immense popularity, and we knew he would sell some tickets. However, in the long run, or possibly even in the short run, winning and playing competitive basketball is the name of the game.

From a purely basketball standpoint we felt that acquiring one of the greatest guards in the NBA was a tremendous step toward bringing New Orleans a winning basketball team. We recognize that one player alone cannot bring a championship but that every great team has a great guard as part of that team. In an expansion situation we felt fortunate to be able to start off with one of the constituent parts of a championship team.

We have been criticized for giving too much, but when the trade is analyzed piece by piece the only real value we gave up was next year's first round draft choice.

Fred Rosenfeld
Owner, New Orleans Jazz

With all my love to my beautiful wife, Cookie, and the kids, Karen, Donna, and Tommy Jr., who put up with all my various moods and the pounding of the typewriter at all hours of the night.

Pete Comes Home

On May 3, 1974, "Pistol" Pete Maravich came home again. Responsible for turning on the entire Bayou country, and eventually the nation during his "showtime" college days at Louisiana State, Maravich returns after a four-year absence with the National Basketball Association's newest baby, the New Orleans Jazz.

But "The Pistol" did not come cheap, in what has been termed "The Louisiana Purchase." The New Orleans franchise, still without players or a coach at the time since the NBA expansion draft was still weeks away, bartered away what amounted to six and possibly eight players to the Atlanta Hawks for the sensational ball-handling wizard.

But all the talk of how much he had given up for "The Pistol" and his patented droopy socks did not disturb Fred Rosenfeld, president of the Jazz, one bit. "The signing of Maravich is the first step in bringing New Orleans the best in NBA basketball," stated the prominent Beverly Hills, California, lawyer.

On the other hand Atlanta Hawks General Manager, Pat Williams, termed the trade a turning point in the future of the Atlanta franchise, which had just completed a disappointing season and was once again switching to a youth movement. "This is a chance to build a franchise that only comes once," he said. "If New Orleans had called the New York Knicks and offered the same deal for Walt Frazier I'd have to feel the Knicks would have jumped at the deal."

Rosenfeld and Maravich: The dynamic duo who hope to bring winning and exciting basketball to New Orleans.

It also marks a bright new start for Maravich, who had never enjoyed true happiness in Atlanta during his four years there, and now returns to the land of his fantastic college career where he became a legend with his droopy socks and behind-the-back passes, not to mention his awesome scoring feats.

It has been a long road from that March day in 1970 when the skinny 21-year-old who averaged better than 44 points a game during his college career at LSU signed a five-year-contract for $1.9 million with Atlanta, becoming the highest paid professional athlete in the land at the time. At that memorable signing, with a barrage of newsmen popping flash bulbs and television lights, Maravich, who scored a record 3,667 points at LSU, said: "This is the thing I've looked forward to. It's like starting out as a freshman again. I wanted to play somewhere in the South, and I'm overly excited about playing in Atlanta."

All was harmony with then Atlanta coach Richie Guerin, who showed his delight by declaring, "I'm very happy. I think Pete will be a big plus to our team and the city of Atlanta."

But things did not quite work out as planned for the Hawks. Not that the Aliquippa, Pennsylvania, youngster did not try, for indeed he did. But he was still cussed and discussed. If the Hawks won, Pete got the credit, and if they lost, he was to blame. He was damned if he did and damned if he did not. But that is the price you pay for fame, and Pete was paying the price.

It all began in Maravich's rookie season. The then powerful Hawks, a veteran team with five black starters, did not take kindly to the brash young kid with the enormous contract. Eventually trades and the passing of time solved that problem. Then came his second season, and again troubles befell the intense young man with the penetrating dark eyes. This time he was knocked out with mononucleosis for nearly a month. His weight fell to 169 pounds from 205, and he never did regain his full strength the rest of the season.

Then early in the 1972-73 season misfortune landed on Pete's doorstep again. This time it was a rare malady called Bell's Palsy. The right side of his face was paralyzed, and he could not close his eyes. His words became slurred, and doctors feared for his career. Fortunately, however, the ailment lasted but three weeks. However, to Pete those three weeks seemed like three years.

Through all the disappointments, illnesses, and pitfalls there were included many good times, and along the way Pete did prove one thing. He was as fine a basketball player as there was in the pro ranks, and he had finally arrived as an NBA superstar.

His arrival came in the 1972-73 season, his third pro year. It was highlighted by his scoring over 2,000 points for the first time, finishing as the NBA's fifth leading scorer with 2,063 points, a 26.1 average per game. He was also selected as the East's All-Star starting guard along with Walt Frazier of the Knicks, and was named to the 10-man NBA All-Pro team at season's end. It was a fitting reward for Pete, who as a rookie poured in 1,880 points and a 23.2 average, then dipped to 1,275 points and a 19.3 average in his second season, when hit by the mono, missing 14 full games.

Again an East All-Star during the 1973-74 campaign, Maravich emerged as the second leading scorer in the league with a 27.7 average, once again soaring over the coveted 2,000-point mark. But the season was an overall disappointment to Pete and the Hawks, who failed "To Soar in 1974," finishing with a 36-48 record and missing the playoffs for the first time since the 1961-62 season.

"There was no personality conflict on the team," says Maravich. And on the day he arrived in New Orleans for the news conference officially announcing the trade which made Pete the only member of the franchise, he reiterated that point. "The trade had nothing to do with team morale," said Pete. "I

Pete's contract lies in front of New Orleans owner Fred Rosenfeld on the day the trade of Maravich to the Jazz is announced.

don't really know the reasons they (Atlanta) wanted to trade me away, but I know they made it evident they didn't want my services anymore. I'm not the type of person that I'm going to make them miserable by staying there."

And so Pete returns to a city only 80 miles down the Mississippi River from Baton Rouge, where he began his famous journey, emerging as the famed "Pistol Pete." And his return is expected to turn New Orleans into a Mardi Gras in short pants for all his followers, old and new alike, when the Jazz takes to the court.

New Orleans Side Of The Trade

Fred Rosenfeld, the dynamic New Orleans owner, had just been awarded the NBA's 18th franchise in early March of 1974 and without blinking quickly turned a $3 phone call into one of the most expensive investments in professional sports.

What he did was lure the magical Maravich away from the capital of the Southeast in Atlanta to New Orleans, a city of famous seafood restaurants, bayous, the Mardi Gras, and the soon to be completed Taj Mahal of sports emporiums, the Superdome. But for the trade to become a reality Maravich had to give his approval since he had a no-trade clause in his contract with Atlanta, and it still had one year remaining. After nearly two weeks of negotiations between both clubs, Maravich and his lawyers, it became a reality.

The talks were initiated, according to first year GM Pat Williams, by New Orleans early in March. Williams, who took over at the start of the 1973 season from the fired Richie Guerin, said he was contacted by Rosenfeld. "The first question Fred asked me was, 'Is Maravich available?' said Williams. That started the ball rolling, and the wheeling and dealing was on. After the transaction was completed, the only thing left was to sign Pete to a New Orleans contract, and it turned out to be rather simple.

Pete's new contract is a three-year pact and is in excess of the one he had at Atlanta which called for $380,000 per year. His only comment on his new contract was to state that New Orleans made it "very interesting" to play for the newest NBA club. "He's happy and we're happy," said Rosenfeld. "We began negotiating about ten days ago with Pete, and we did not have any difficulty. We took Pete, and Pete came to us because we mutually understood each other."

Rosenfeld went on to say that, "We're going to have some of the top basketball people in the country associated with our team, and they feel Pete can do the things necessary to contribute to a winning climate. They feel Pete can be the cornerstone of a championship team."

Maravich has heard that said of him before, being hailed as the savior of the Hawks in their bid for a NBA title when he first joined Atlanta as a rookie. But after guiding the Hawks to the playoffs during the 1972-73 season where they eventually lost to the Boston Celtics, four games to two, Maravich also received most of the blame—unjustly—for the Hawks' poor showing in 1973-74.

"No one man ever won a championship, and no one man ever lost one," he explains simply. But he again pointed out that Atlanta's willingness to trade him had nothing to do with team morale, which Hawks coach Cotton Fitzsimmons quickly agreed. "When I first signed (as a rookie)," says Maravich, "players jumped, kicked, and quit in Atlanta. But our problems this year had nothing to do with jealousies. There were no player fallouts. That was all gone. Injuries hurt us this year."

Maravich then switched his thoughts to his new club, saying he feels that New Orleans "has a great chance" of being competitive immediately. "The people behind the New Orleans franchise are basketball knowledgeable, and this is one ingredient all championship teams have. With knowledgeable management, it shouldn't take long. I think we might have a chance of getting to the championship quicker in New Orleans than Atlanta does," added Pete, taking a poke at his former club. "When I do get that championship ring, I'll quit," he says. "I'll have had it with basketball," something Pete has said many times in the past.

Williams, who has since left Atlanta for a similar post with Philadelphia, on the other hand, defends the deal, saying, "It's a new franchise for us. If I were general manager of any other team in the NBA, I would have made the same trade for any player, with the possible exception of Kareem Abdul-Jabbar or Bob Lanier."

Fitzsimmons is equally adamant in defending the move. "This gives us a chance. It was the only trade I would make. I never have believed in trading a player just for the sake of making a trade," he said.

But there is still the feeling around the NBA that the Hawks pulled off a coup. It is something that cannot be evaluated, however, for many years to come. Only time will tell.

Detroit coach Ray Scott, however, was overheard telling Fitzsimmons at a league meeting during the summer, his thoughts. "Hey, Cotton, you're just like the muggers in New York. I understand you come out after 11 p.m. every night, wearing a mask and a gun."

But Fitzsimmons refused Scott's bait by defending both sides of the deal. "I think that (trade) really has to be considered a compliment to Pete Maravich," said Fitzsimmons, who also shrugs off the rumors of a grudge between himself and Maravich. Yet one has to wonder. "Not as far as I'm concerned," says Fitzsimmons. "But I have not talked to Pete since the end of the season. I did call him, but he prefers not to talk to me."

But he does admit that their relationship was not what you might call "chummy." Fitzsimmons also maintains that Pete's two-day suspension earlier in the season had nothing to do with the trade.

"The suspension was for something that happened off the court," says Fitzsimmons. "And it was for something people have been suspended for before. I have not, and will not talk about it, because it has to do with a player's image. If it was something that had happened in a game or practice, then it would be a different matter.

"After the suspension, however," admits Fitzsimmons, "our relationship deteriorated. It wasn't really anything I did or anything Pete did. It's like when my father used to discipline me. Well, for awhile, I was mad at him."

The Atlanta coach also said he felt Maravich's problems were further complicated by the fact that he was being blamed for the Hawks' having a losing season. "We did not win," said Fitzsimmons, "and when you are a star player, you are sometimes referred to as the difference, whether that is true or not. I think Pete lumped some things together and said he was

New Orleans owner Fred Rosenfeld appears to be leading the band (Jazz?). Actually, he is answering a question at the news conference announcing the signing of Pete.

being blamed for our season.

"But," says Cotton firmly, "I think it is an unfair rap. Pete came out of college as the best scorer in history. The Hawks signed him on that basis. Maybe the Hawks and Maravich expected too much. I know I fought that for two years. Pete tried to do everything I asked. But if you have run down the court and shoot every time you have the ball from the first time you touched a ball, then it is very difficult to change that," he said.

Can Pete change his style?

"I don't know," says Fitzsimmons. "A player has to work hard at it. I think he has the talent to do anything in basketball.

Atlanta General Manager Pat Williams, who broke the trade news to Maravich. Williams has since left Atlanta for a similar post with Philadelphia.

Being traded was, I feel, a traumatic experience for him. At least that's what I understand from his reaction. I know this: he can make up his mind to go to New Orleans and do everything possible to prove the Atlanta Hawks were wrong in trading him. I hope he can adjust with a new team and be successful."

And Pete's success will not only mean success for the Jazz and the league, it will undoubtedly pack them in at the Omni in

Atlanta when the Jazz and Maravich return to Hawk territory. To that, Fitzsimmons readily agrees. "Maravich is the No. 1 individual draw in basketball," he says. "He appeals to a lot of people. He sells tickets. I consider him No. 1 in that respect. Jabbar is second. Jerry West has dropped some, but he's third. Bill Walton coming in will also be a great individual ticket seller."

Fitzsimmons had still another compliment for Maravich, knowing full well that "The Pistol" will be returning to Atlanta as the enemy with venom in his heart. "The trade was certainly not a slam at Pete," said Fitzsimmons. "We couldn't have traded him to any other club for what we got. It should make Pete feel real good to know that he was traded for at least six players and possibly eight. Remember, Wilt Chamberlain was traded for only three."

Yet he still admits that both teams took a gamble. "But if our gamble pays off, we should be a strong team for many years. And maybe Pete will change, to prove he can do it. He may say, 'I can change, and I will change.'"

Maravich is not saying whether he will or not, but he does have his own ideas on shooting down the trade in the only way he knows how, by winning basketball games.

"If we win 30 games, which is not impossible," says Pete, "that will screw up the whole trade. That's what I'm out to do. The following year we switch places in the draft. If we finish higher, then we get their place and pick ahead of them. Wouldn't that be nice?" he said smiling, similar to the cat getting ready to pounce on the mouse.

Pete has the motivation for revenge and his feelings go all the way back to the time when the trade rumors began to emerge. Maravich has voiced his displeasure over the way the Hawks went about making the deal, claiming it was done behind his back and adding that he was lied to by the Hawks. "I would have liked it if the Hawks had been honest with me and said, 'Pete, we're thinking of trading you to New Orleans, and they have a great feeling for you.' That would have been fine. But to do it all in one day, the way they did it, that left a bad taste.

"I think many of the fans wanted me to stay, and I don't think the Hawks dealt honestly with me. I, for one, think they could have told me instead of doing it all behind my back.

"But after everything is said and done," says Maravich, "everybody has his side to the trade. I know I was not wanted in the organization, and I also know the reasons behind why I'm no longer in Atlanta. But I have to go where my business takes me, and my business takes me to New Orleans."

A couple of days later, a calmer Maravich viewed the trade again in a different light. "I like Atlanta, but I wasn't in a position to say I'm not going to New Orleans, I'm staying in Atlanta. I know I had a clause in my contract, but being realistic I wasn't wanted by management, so I moved on.

"The New Orleans franchise happened to come into being, and I wanted to stay in the South, and New Orleans is the South," he said.

"Basketball is a cutthroat business, but I'm happy with the trade. I feel fortunate in going to New Orleans. When you have the right people in the organization, you have a better chance of winning. I don't consider this club an expansion club, and I don't think it'll take us three to five years to become a winner.

"We're going to be playing in the most magnificent arena in the world—the Superdome—it might not be ready until January, but until then we'll be playing in Civic Auditorium," said Pete. "I've played there in college, and it's a great place to play."

He also admits that he's working hard to get off to a fast start in his new home. "For the first time in my life," says Pete, "I've been running four miles a week all summer and I'm working pretty hard. I have a program of weights and hope to play at between 215 and 220 pounds this year. I can use the weight, and it will make me faster, stronger, and quicker. I'll be in the best shape of my entire career."

"I have this feeling about New Orleans, and I'm going to do the best I can for the New Orleans team," says Pete, who undoubtedly is out to prove Atlanta wrong in trading him away.

Before The Trade

Pete has revenge in his heart now, but when the trade rumors originally broke earlier in April "The Pistol" had to make up his own mind on whether to go, stay in Atlanta, or even retire.

"I really can't tolerate any more deceit and deception on the part of the coach and the present administration," said Maravich on April 25, the day the trade rumors surfaced.

Pete said he met with Hawks management a week earlier, and there was no mention of a trade. But a day later, said Maravich, Hawks president John Wilcox contacted his lawyers in Pittsburgh and told him the Hawks had been negotiating a deal with New Orleans for a month.

"It just makes me feel that the whole time I was talking with those people, trying to get our problems worked out, I made myself look like a fool," said Pete.

That same night Maravich said General Manager Williams called him and asked to meet with him. "I told him sure, to come on out to my apartment," said Maravich.

"He came and said he liked my place, asked how I was, then said, 'I'll lay my cards right on the table. With your approval we would like to trade you to New Orleans. We got a great deal.'"

"I was shocked," said Maravich. "I have never wanted to leave Atlanta, but I guess it's looking like I might have to...But I really don't know anything yet for sure."

Although it would take nearly two weeks for Maravich to

make up his mind, the handwriting was there for all to see. All that was needed was for Pete to give his approval.

For the young man who took up the game at the age of four and had spent all of his growing up years with a basketball tucked under his arms, Maravich had a lot of thinking to do. The decision was his, and his alone.

He still had one year left on his original five-year pact with the Hawks, and it contained an all important no-trade agreement.

"I haven't made up my mind yet," said Pete at the time. "I have some people to talk to and a lot of things to think over before I reach a decision."

First a meeting with the owners of the New Orleans franchise was set up, with Pete saying he would "probably meet them sometime in the next two weeks."

Money was not the prime factor in the deal, he said.

"I'm not in basketball for money anymore. That may be easy for me to say. But I got where I am because I busted my rear end to get there.

"My only goal in basketball now is to play on a championship team. If I go to an expansion team, then I have to feel the chances of doing that are reduced. But then, with new management, a new team—who knows for sure what will happen? That's the kind of thing I have to think over and consider before I make a decision."

The thing that still irked Maravich was the way the Hawks did all their maneuvering behind his back, he says.

"I tried to be forthright with people, and I just wasn't prepared for deception."

One of Maravich's attorneys, Les Zittrain, who helped "The Pistol" renegotiate his $1.9 million contract with the Hawks when the prolific scorer turned pro, agreed.

"We had asked to talk with the Hawks two weeks before anything was mentioned about a trade," said Zittrain. "There were several things to discuss. No shouting or demands, or anything like that. Just some things to help get next season off on the proper foot. There was no mention of a trade. We had a nice talk, or at least I thought it was nice, until later."

Zittrain said he had not even heard of the rumors of a possible trade. He went to Hawks president John Wilcox in an attempt to clear the air and Wilcox stated: "Pete has a no-trade contract. And there has been no occasion to talk to him or his attorney about it. No discussion has been made on those lines whatsoever."

Ten days later the rumors became fact. "Unbeknownst to us," said Zittrain, "the Hawks had been working a month on the deal with New Orleans. And to put it mildly, it caught us by surprise. Pete was upset and undecided. He was upset over the way it was handled and undecided on whether he would

John Wilcox, president of the Hawks, who approved the trade of "The Pistol" to New Orleans.

approve the trade. We'll probably sit and cool it for a little bit. Then we'll have another meeting. But Pete can take care of himself."

Obviously the move to New Orleans would add dollars to Maravich's bank account, but this was not the primary concern, said Zittrain echoing Pete's words. "There is no way we can be hurt financially in this thing," he said. "As a matter of fact we could make Atlanta renegotiate and come up with money right now. But our complaint with the Hawks is not economic. It is with the manner in which this has been handled."

Zittrain then hinted that the fans in Atlanta may have a strong influence in helping Maravich come to a decision.

"I wonder, seriously, how the sports fans would react if Pete left," he said. "Would they say good riddance, or would they say here's a kid who has put out all he can to bring Atlanta a winner?"

One who felt the move to New Orleans would be an excellent one for Pete was Press Maravich, his father and former coach at LSU, who currently coaches at Appalachian State University in South Carolina.

"I think it would be a break for Pete," said Papa Maravich. "But I feel he's capable of making his own decision. I know Pete has a no-trade contract, but I don't know what he intends to do. I feel it would be a break for him to go with a new franchise.

"Like I told him recently," said Press. "When the flesh peddlers get behind closed doors, you can be a Babe Ruth or a Hank Aaron, but you had better keep your suitcase packed."

Papa then noted that he felt Pete was with what started, "as a good organization up until the time the team was sold. When he was playing for me, I utilized his talents."

Pete, whose talents are shooting and passing a basketball in a manner never seen before in college or the pros, drew many critics with his play, but Pete answers those charges with some anger. "As for my critics who say Pete Maravich does this and does that, (that he) passes behind his back, I just say they're stupid. I used to lay back and kill people with kindness but no more.

"I started playing basketball at four, and I knew all about it when I was five. When I was 12 I knew I would play in the

Pete during his All-Star year 1972-73. Those were the good times, and there were no thoughts of trading him then.

NBA, so it was no surprise to me when I signed in this league," said Pete, letting off some steam. "That's not being cocky, it's just confidence. I played every day, eight to ten hours a day, and I knew I could do things other kids couldn't do. I sacrificed a lot of things to play basketball. But that's all I ever wanted to do. I think it was worth it."

It was pointed out that the pressure on him would grow in intensity now that he would be performing once again before people where he first began his legendary scoring feats.

"The pressure is always there, and I think there will be more this coming year," agreed Pete. "If you look back at my career, it built up year after year. I try to handle it within myself. I have come to expect it. Pressure is pressure. I've grown up with it. I've lived with pressure all my life. But I think I've grown up and matured so I can handle it. It's never gotten to the point where I can't handle it."

And so the four-year love-hate affair in Atlanta had ended for Pete Maravich. It had been a long, disheartening process of disillusionment. From the moment when Pete, rosy-cheeked and innocent, signed his Hawks contract with all the surrounding hoopla at a plush Atlanta hotel, until now, the marriage had not worked out as planned.

His first game as a rookie Hawk in regular season was a nationally-televised affair against Milwaukee which boasted Kareem-Abdul Jabbar and Oscar Robertson. But those two proven NBA superstars drew virtually no billing opposed to the young kid just out of college with the floppy hair and piercing dark eyes.

That was the day when the Hawks management stated: "We paid Maravich two million dollars in salary, bonus, insurance deals, and real estate, but we started getting it back today."

Two million dollars! Only two years before, another $1 million could have bought the entire franchise. That is what Tom Cousins bought the Hawks for when the team came over from St. Louis in 1969.

Maravich drew the fans to the games, but the Hawks expected him to pack the stands for every game, something that was virtually impossible since much of the rest of the Hawks' cast was shy of being a championship contender.

And so Pete will now place his exciting wares on display for the New Orleans fans, who hopefully will be turned on by his "showtime" act and will be patient with the newest kid on the NBA block.

"Any player is expendable," said Pete. "I know that. But there were a lot of things that happened in Atlanta. There were a lot of injuries, but that wasn't the whole thing. Really, though, I wouldn't like to comment on it."

What Pete was not elaborating upon, but which may have helped in sending him on his way, was that "happening" in February, 1974, when he drew the wrath of Coach Cotton Fitzsimmons and received a two-day suspension.

That could have been the beginning of the end for Maravich in Atlanta.

Suspension

The behind-the-scenes maneuvering which sent Maravich to New Orleans, with the Hawks allegedly receiving more than Napoleon got when he sold the entire Louisiana Purchase to Thomas Jefferson, may have begun in earnest that Sunday night in Houston. The exact date was February 3, 1974, and the Hawks lost to the Houston Rockets 123-112 that evening. But the loss was incidental to what occurred during and after the contest.

In that game Maravich had to be restrained from going after referee Jim Capers in the first half. Teammates Herm Gilliam and Lou Hudson did the restraining with Hudson coming out of Maravich's wild-arm-swinging with a bloody nose.

Then in the fourth quarter and the Hawks trailing, Fitzsimmons benched "The Pistol" for the final 9½ minutes of the game. Fitzsimmons later said he felt "Pete did not have his head in the game" after the incident with the referee.

All appeared peaceful as the Hawks returned to Atlanta the next morning by plane, but Tuesday morning a statement was released to the media by the Hawks saying Maravich had been suspended indefinitely for disciplinary reasons. Not one of the reasons was given however.

Speculation abounded about the suspension, which made headlines around the nation, but to this day it is just that, speculation. No one, not Fitzsimmons nor Maravich, has ever mentioned the reasons for the suspension.

Some of the alleged reasons were:

—The incident with the referee on Sunday.

—An argument with Fitzsimmons after the game.

—An incident at the team's hotel in Houston during the week hours.

—Words with Fitzsimmons on the return flight from Houston.

"A lot of guessing has been done in the last 48 hours," said Fitzsimmons on Tuesday, referring to the reasons for the suspension. "But nobody has come close," he said.

The disturbance in the Houston hotel after the game appears to be the closest to the truth, however.

"I haven't talked to Pete since Tuesday," said Fitzsimmons after the announcement, saying he had set up a meeting with Maravich for the following Thursday concerning his reinstatement to the club. "He is to meet with me before practice that day," said the blond coach who was in his second year as head man of the Hawks.

"I told Pete Tuesday if he wanted to, to meet me before practice Thursday. I don't want anybody back who does not want to come back. He can stay out as long as he wants to. It's up to him," declared the peppery 5-foot-9 Fitzsimmons.

Meanwhile, in the absence of Pete, the Hawks reeled off two consecutive victories, and speculation arose that maybe Atlanta was better off without Maravich. But Fitzsimmons and the rest of the club knew better.

Pete showed up Thursday for the meeting with Fitzsimmons, and after a 45-minute discussion between the two at Morehouse College in Atlanta where the Hawks occasionally practice, Fitzsimmons announced:

"The suspension is lifted. You can't talk to Pete, because he's not available, and he's not available because he doesn't want to be. Pete will play in Philadelphia tomorrow night."

Fitzsimmons then said, "There are no hard feelings at all. I feel bad about having to suspend him, and he feels worse than anyone. I think just being suspended was embarrassing enough for him without being questioned about it. He will play Friday.

"We could lose to Philadelphia," Fitzsimmons continued, "and if we do I don't want people to think it's because Pete played. One player cannot get you beat. One player does not win. We were able to win without Pete in two games, but we also won without Lou Hudson. So why put it all on Pete."

And so the Hawks jetted up to the city of Brotherly Love, and you guessed it—they lost. But Fitzsimmons was true to his word, coming to the rescue of Maravich.

"I wanted to win for everybody, but I especially wanted to win for Pete," said the coach. "It's easy for you guys (sportswriters) to point the finger. All you have to do is read the papers all over. They'll say. 'Maravich Back, Hawks Lose.'" But Fitzsimmons emphatically pointed out: "We didn't lose because Pete came back."

Maravich did not start the game, entering at the beginning of the second quarter and finishing the night with only eight points, taking but nine shots in his 26 minutes of action as the Hawks lost 104-84.

"You guys make me feel like I've been out for six months," said a relaxed Pete after the game. "The only thing that bothered me was that I wasn't in my best physical condition. I hadn't touched a ball since we played in Houston on Sunday."

Pete, who incidentally had never been suspended before or since, still remains mum on the subject.

"I really have no comment on it," he says. And he still hasn't. Asked then about his future in Atlanta, Pete said: "I don't know whether I'm going to stay or not."

Three months, to the day, he was no longer a member of the Atlanta Hawks. Maybe he knew something then. At the time of Pete's suspension, rumors flew about Atlanta with even a pair of psychics getting into the act by predicting early retirement for "The Pistol."

"He's going to retire," said noted psychic Evelyn Monahan. "It seems strange, 'Pistol Pete' and all that, but I see him retiring after a season and a half or sooner."

And you know something, she was half right. Maravich did retire from the Hawks.

Now it is the fans of New Orleans who will be blessed with seeing Pete in person, a player gifted with cobra-quick reflexes—one of the most exciting players to come along in NBA history. But his free wheeling individualistic style did not please everyone and apparently conflicted with Fitzsimmons' ideas as a strict disciplinarian.

A disgusted Pete getting a bit of advice from Coach Cotton Fitzsimmons during a timeout. The two failed to communicate after Pete's two-day suspension.

"I've found that most professional basketball players need and actually want discipline," explained Fitzsimmons. "If a coach doesn't demand that things be done a certain way, he's going to have a hard time. You can't treat them like children, but you can lead them in the right direction."

But on the other side of the argument, there is only one Pete Maravich, a player who draws national headlines and attention whenever he steps on the court. He is idolized by millions of youngsters around the country, and Pete's artistic face can be seen adorning the front pages of magazine covers and on television commercials at most any time.

Noted columnist Furman Bisher of the *Atlanta Journal* once wrote that what Pete Maravich needs "Is a basketball league of his own. Or the Harlem Globetrotters for a supporting cast. The NBA simply isn't good enough for his act. He plays a game in such a way it seems he invented it. He is incredibly blessed with the features that make a man a basketball player.

"Quick hands, swift feet, vision that seems to have a range of 360 degrees, and a touch for finding the basket. His act is the kind that needs only extras," Bisher wrote. "It's the kind you find in center ring in a tent."

And Fitzsimmons is the first to admit that trying to make Maravich fit into his scheme of things was his fault.

"Part of it was my mistake," says Fitzsimmons. "I went against my own game these two years trying to make it work with Pete. I've always played a controlled offense, work the ball into the big men. I've tried it this way. It won't work. I'm going back to my old game."

And so Maravich takes his game of improvisation to New Orleans, with a bright outlook, brand new franchise, teammates, coach, and Superdome.

It's A New Ballgame

On May 20, 1974, Pete Maravich finally found out who his new teammates would be. That was the day that the New Orleans franchise took 15 players from the other 17 established NBA clubs. Atlanta had its pick of the top forward and guard in the draft as part of the dividends in the Maravich deal.

The Hawks chose guard Dean Meminger from the New York Knicks and forward Bob Kauffman, a 6-foot-8 forward from Buffalo.

Then New Orleans made its selections:

—Dennis Awtrey, 26, center, 6-10, 240 pounds, 4 year pro from Chicago.

—Walt Bellamy, 35, center, 6-11, 245, 13 year pro from Atlanta.

—Jim Barnett, 30, guard, 6-4, 175, 8 year pro from Golden State.

—Nate Hawthorne, 24, guard, 6-4, 195, 1 year pro from Los Angeles.

—Stu Lantz, 28, guard, 6-3, 175, 6 year pro from Detroit.

—Louie Nelson, 23, guard, 6-3, 190, 1 year pro from Washington.

—John Block, 30, forward, 6-10, 210, 8 year pro from Kansas City-Omaha.

—Barry Clemens, 31, forward, 6-7, 219, 9 year pro from Cleveland.

—E. C. Coleman, 24, forward, 6-8, 225, 1 year pro from Houston.

—Lamar Green, 27, forward, 6-8, 220, 5 year pro from

Walt Bellamy setting a pick for Pete who is getting ready to unload his jumper against Houston. The two will be teammates again this year with The Jazz.

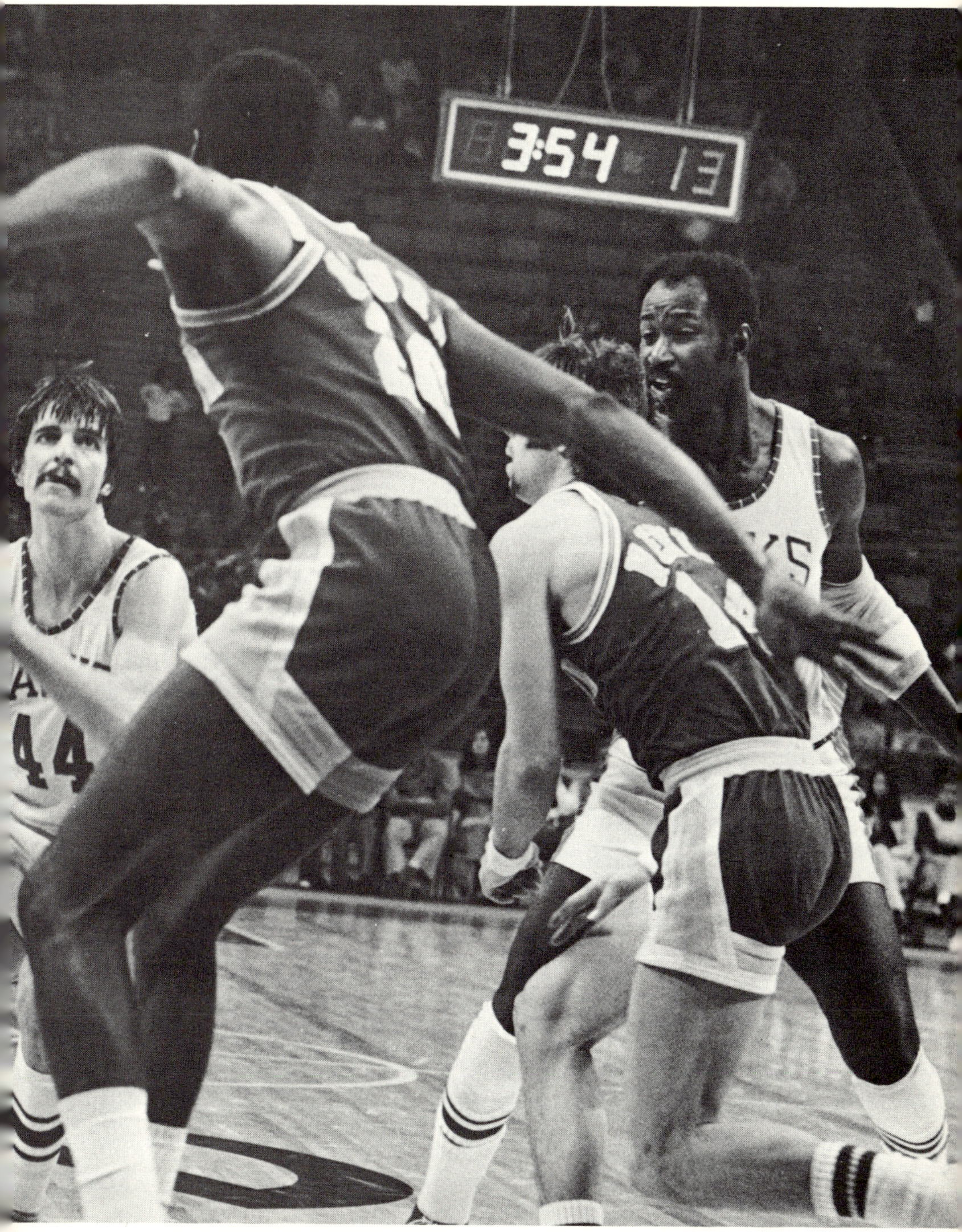
3:54
13
44

Phoenix.

—Ollie Johnson, 25, forward, 6-6, 200, 2 year pro from Portland.

—Toby Kimball, 32, forward, 6-8, 242, 8 year pro from Philadelphia.

—Steve Kuberski, 27, forward, 6-8, 220, 5 year pro from Boston.

—Curtis Perry, 26, forward, 6-7, 220, 3 year pro from Milwaukee.

—Bud Stallworth, 24, forward, 6-5, 190, 2 year pro from Seattle.

Rosenfeld, the New Orleans owner, said he was "extremely excited, delighted, and thrilled" about his 15 picks. And he is particularly jubilant when he refers to the man he feels will team with Maravich in the back court—Stu Lantz.

"Stu, along with Maravich, gives us arguably the best back court in basketball. It's a hell of an achievement for us to claim this," he said.

Lantz, a six-year veteran, averaged 8.9 points last season with Detroit.

"We feel we should be able to exceed the record number of wins by an expansion team, which is 33," says Rosenfeld. "We were the only team selecting from this pool of players, and if we don't exceed the best previous mark maybe that might suggest we aren't doing things correctly." The best previous mark was Chicago's 33-48 record in 1966-67.

The man doing the ground work for New Orleans in the draft was Bill Bertka, hired as vice-president of operations—better known as the GM or general manager. He came to New Orleans from Los Angeles where he was director of player personnel and chief scout.

"We feel we've achieved the balance we wanted," said Bertka. "We picked each player after considering his style and how it compliments the style of the others selected. It was done on a team concept. We feel we also have a balance between youth and experience. We hope with a little daylight now some of these people can develop into fine players. I think we've laid the ground work for future success."

Steve Kuberski, Boston's top forward reserve, said he thought "we're already better off than a lot of other teams in the league. I'm happy to be in New Orleans."

Lantz said he was particularly anxious to play with Maravich. "After seeing and playing against Pete for four years I can't contradict that statement," said Lantz upon hearing that owner Rosenfeld said he felt the duo would be one of the best in the league. "Maravich is a helluva start in that direction himself," said Lantz.

Kuberski was also excited at the opportunity of playing with "The Pistol."

"As far as playing with Pete, anybody who's been around the league long enough to know talent knows he can play. The rap against him has been his defense, and I don't think he's ever been called upon to really play defense before. I don't see any reason why he shouldn't fit in. He's an exceptional talent."

Another teammate of Pete's will be Walt Bellamy, the big veteran center who has played with Maravich for the past 3½ years in Atlanta. Bellamy also voiced his displeasure at the Hawks for dealings in which he considered "unsportsmanlike conduct."

Bellamy's act of rebellion against the Hawks, after being selected by New Orleans in the expansion draft, was to call a news conference of his own—nothing extravagant—in fact it was held in a black section of Atlanta, taking place on a street corner near a busy intersection.

"Bells" claimed that "Atlanta forced a player (himself) on New Orleans. They came up with a scheme where they forced New Orleans to take over my contract."

The articulate Bellamy, a 13-year NBA veteran, and only one of eight players in the history of the league to pour in more than 20,000 points, said he was being placed "in a forced retirement." He claimed it was due to a lack of communications between himself and the Hawks and several times at the conference referred to Fitzsimmons as "a con artist" and "con man."

Although Bellamy has since "unretired," he says he had heard rumors that Atlanta was going to force New Orleans to take him in the expansion draft as part of the Pete Maravich deal. So first it was Maravich, who was upset at the Hawks management, claiming underhanded dealings, and now it was Bellamy.

Some of Pete's new teammates with the Jazz, who came to

New Orleans in the NBA expansion draft.

"I really don't know what to say," said Atlanta GM Pat Williams. "He's not being forced to retire. He's New Orleans property. Bellamy was no longer a Hawk when New Orleans drafted him."

But Williams did confirm that Bellamy had come to him and asked about Atlanta's plans for him in the future along with his $196,000 per year salary, which still had a year remaining.

"We told Bells at that time that it was impossible to tell him what our plans were," said Williams.

But Williams maintains that Bellamy "was not part of the deal with New Orleans, as such. The deal was that we could freeze seven players and tell New Orleans what players to take in the expansion draft," explained Williams. "I called Bellamy after the draft and gave him a complete report of the facts."

Now Walt Bellamy is added to the list along with Pete Maravich who have more than ample reason to lay in ambush while eagerly awaiting confrontations with the Hawks.

A short while after the expansion draft was completed, New Orleans named its coach. The Jazz announced that Scotty Robertson, a local favorite who had coached at Louisiana Tech for the past ten years and in Louisiana high schools previous to that, would be guiding the New Orleans franchise in its debut.

"Scotty, going in at least, plays the kind of game we think wins in the NBA," owner Rosenfeld said upon naming Robertson. "He's got a toughness and discipline about him. He's the kind of guy we think we can win with."

The question of Robertson, an unknown quantity in the pro ranks, arose, but Rosenfeld was quick to defend his choice of the virtually unknown 44-year-old.

"We hire a coach at this stage, and unless it's one of those guys who are proven NBA winners, it's a gamble. After you get past New York coach Red Holtzman, Larry Costello of Milwaukee, Bill Sharman—Los Angeles, and Dick Motta— Chicago, there are maybe a couple of guys who'll win for you," said Rosenfeld. "We knew we were not going to get any of the fellows I just listed, and we didn't want to go to a guy who bounced around the NBA losing here, and there, and then give him a chance to lose for us.

"So we thought we would go into the colleges," said Rosenfeld. "And Scotty has a pretty good record at Tech. You like to look to a guy who has had success in every environment he's been in, even though it may not be the big league.

"Scotty, at every level in which he coached, was very successful. You like to see that pattern. That's why we've got Scotty."

Suppose superstar Pete Maravich is in need of discipline, how would that be handled?

"I don't want to get involved and talk about how we are going to discipline Pete," says Rosenfeld. "I think that is totally nonproductive, really, at this stage to say, 'Yeah, if Pete doesn't do it, we are going to bench him.'

"But I'll tell you something. I'm convinced that you do bench a player who is not playing the game the way it has to be played."

Maravich has been accused by some of not being a team player, simply a show-off, more interested in doing his own thing. Rosenfeld emphatically disagrees.

"Look at what happened to Earl Monroe, who was supposed to be the country's greatest playground player," he says. "He wasn't supposed to be able to play with the Knicks. They pass, cut, set screens, pick, and do all those things that Monroe was not used to. But look at Earl now. He fits in because he knows that with Holtzman, he's not going to play otherwise.

"Maravich has the skills, the ability to play well in this league," says Rosenfeld. "There is no part of the game he can't play. He can play defense, believe me. You never beat one man when there is another guy there to pick up the slack. Pete Maravich understands all those things. He wants to do those things."

To begin with, Rosenfeld says he has signed Maravich to a standard three-year NBA player contract. There are not any "no cut" or "no trade" clauses in Pete's contract, such as he had in Atlanta.

"We are just not going to do it," says Rosenfeld. "Here we are with an established superstar like Pete who will be coming to camp like anyone else."

And significantly, says Rosenfeld, Maravich himself pacified the only serious breakdown in negotiations between Pete's lawyers and himself, who were insisting that a no-cut, no-trade contract be included in their demands.

"We actually got up from the table and were leaving," said Rosenfeld. "It was Pete who prevailed on his attorneys. He was willing to come to New Orleans without the added provisions. The fact that Pete agreed to this is significant. Here's a kid who had all that security saying, 'Look, I want to play your way. I'm going to do things you have to do to win.'

"In Pete we've gotten one of the most prolific scorers in the whole league," says Rosenfeld. "And we're not going to pick up anyone like that in the college draft or expansion draft."

The owner agreed that the two critical areas of the trade will not necessarily be the 1974 and 1975 first round college picks which New Orleans owes Atlanta as part of the trade for Pete—but the possibility of Atlanta getting high picks on the first rounds of the 1976 and 1977 draft by switching the selection order with New Orleans.

So far, to obtain Maravich, it has cost New Orleans, Dean Meminger, Bob Kauffman, and the University of Utah's Mike Sojourner, Atlanta's choice which they received from New Orleans. The Hawks also receive New Orleans' No. 1 college choice in 1975 and has the option of taking either New Orleans' top draft picks in 1976 and 1977 or their own, whichever is higher. The Jazz also gave the Hawks their second round draft choices in 1975 and 1976.

But Rosenfeld adamantly defends the trade.

"We have the philosophy that we gave almost nothing to get the most dynamic player in the game of basketball," stated Rosenfeld. "This year we had the tenth pick (Atlanta took Sojourner). What are you going to get in the way of talent, and what kind of price would you have to pay for a No. 10 draft choice? Next year, okay, we gave up something. But after that, we didn't.

"I'd like to emphasize that we still have a first-round pick in 1976 and 1977. On paper, unless something unexpected develops, the Hawks probably won't be much better than us," added Rosenfeld.

"So, what did we give to get a proven quantity who can provide the people here with exciting basketball? The second-round choices don't bother us, and the two players Atlanta got

Pete has grown a mustache again and the beginning of a beard while awaiting his debut with the Jazz.

from the expansion list (Meminger and Kauffman) aren't going to be anything spectacular compared to Pete Maravich."

And so New Orleans finally had a team with Maravich as the ringleader and 16 others who played in the NBA, including Mel Counts, picked up from Los Angeles for a future draft choice. In the college draft they chose virtual unknowns with their top pick being No. 2 choice, forward Aaron James, a product of nearby Grambling.

All that was left now, was picking a nickname for the newest kid on the NBA block, and that was left to the fans. And that came on June 7 when the name Jazz was selected from over 6,500 entries.

"We wanted a name that would tie into what this city is all about," said Rosenfeld. "People here take jazz seriously. We hope that's how they'll take their basketball team."

Forty of the over 6,500 entries chose the name Jazz, and a drawing was held to determine the winner, who received a free trip to Phoenix for the 1975 NBA All-Star game. Jazz, defined in the dictionary as "collective improvisation," seemed an appropriate name, said Rosenfeld.

He could also have had Maravich in mind, who with a basketball in his hands is one of the greatest improvisers around.

Pete, The Improvisor

At different times during his illustrious career Pete Maravich has stated the following: he was thinking of retiring; would not retire until he won a championship; liked playing in Atlanta; did not like playing in Atlanta; spoke to reporters; and did not talk to reporters. The subject of retirement surfaced again for the umpteenth time in February, 1974.

"I'm giving serious consideration to ending my playing career when my five-year contract ends next year," Pete said at that time. "I'm not saying that I definitely would quit after next year," reversing direction like a scatback in football, "I'd be a fool to say that. But right now, I have to say I am considering it. I've said that before."

Pete's latest outburst was triggered by a nationally televised CBS sports special shown earlier in the month.

"I was misled by the people doing that. I was interviewed by them, and I thought it was a program concerning the entire Atlanta Hawks basketball team," said Pete. "But when they got through editing and cutting it, it looked like it was done just to show that I can make mistakes on a basketball court. It looked like it was all just negative."

He said one of the ideas of the program was to point out the poor attendance at Hawks home games.

"They showed a scene of almost nobody in the stands," said a somewhat peeved Maravich. "But they had done it an hour and a half before the game started. I know we're not drawing a lot of people this season, but I told the television people I thought the smallest crowd we've had this year was around 5,400."

Maravich said that was the kind of reporting that "has happened to me before, but when it gets on a national basis like that. Here's a man who has seen me play maybe two times in his life, and all of a sudden he's an expert on every facet of pro basketball. And people believe him. Just like if Walter Cronkite says something. People believe he knows what he's talking about."

Pete said in the game shown on the program, "I scored 33 points, had 15 rebounds, and 7 assists. But the program emphasized me throwing the ball away two times. I can make a mistake. I can have a bad game—any player can—but I'm not the Atlanta Hawks. The Atlanta Hawks are 12 players, 2 coaches, and a trainer. I'm just one of them."

He then reemphasized the fact that he would no longer be the scapegoat anymore.

"I've been one before, and I'm not going to be again. I've never stepped on anybody's toes in four years here," he said. "Mine have been stepped on a lot. I don't have to put up with it. Who needs it? They say the Hawks are $160,000 in the red because of me. They say the Hawks are losing because of me. They say the Hawks will never win because of me. I don't believe any of that, but some people do, and it gets publicized. It makes sensational stories."

It is no wonder then, that Maravich has some misgivings when talking to the press.

About the time of the TV program, the rumors started to surface, saying Maravich would be placed on the trading block. The Hawks' management did not deny it, saying that any player would be available if the right deal came along. Then Fitzsimmons confirmed it by saying, "If this group proves it can't win, then you have to make changes."

Had Maravich, himself, considered the possibility of leaving Atlanta? Apparently not, according to his remarks.

"I like Atlanta. I like where I live," he said. "This is where I wanted to play."

But the feeling persisted that Maravich could not fit into the brand of basketball that the conservative Fitzsimmons demanded of his teams. Again, however, Fitzsimmons disagreed.

"Pete Maravich can play any kind of basketball he wants to. He's a great player, and great players can do what they want to."

That was something Maravich and Fitzsimmons could agree to.

"Last year we won, and nobody talked about what kind of basketball I was playing," Pete said. "I can play any kind, any style of basketball in the world. This season we started out like gangbusters. We blew people out. Then Herm Gilliam gets hurt. Lou Hudson gets hurt. Walt Bellamy gets hurt. I get hurt. We got inexperienced people playing. All the kind of things that can make you have a bad season.

"But I read or hear it's because I don't play the right kind of basketball," sighed Pete. "Last year it was all right, and I have not changed my game. I think maybe the news media changes, depending on whether you win or lose."

But Maravich has come to expect the criticism as part of his life which is the price he paid when he placed his signature on the dotted line with the Hawks in 1970.

Another time, only a week earlier in New York, Maravich was quoted as saying he would definitely quit after the 1974-75 season. "I know nobody will believe this, but it's only one more year for me," Pete was quoted in the *New York Post*.

Fitzsimmons, for one, did not take the news seriously, saying "Pete was putting the guy on."

And the reporter should have taken the hint when he asked Pete what he would do if he retired. "I'll take Jack Palance's place," said the mischievous Maravich. "I'm the villain. I'll make a great villain."

Teammate Jim Washington also had an interesting view of the proceedings.

"The way things have been going, losing and all that, I feel like retiring after every defeat," the personable forward said. "And I'm sure Pete feels the same way. But there will be a new game, a new victory, and a new season and a new enthusiasm," putting the whole situation into perspective.

"All players go through those phases and thoughts," Washington said. "The only thing I've heard Pete say along those lines is that he'd quit after being on a championship team. But that, too, is tentative. You win one championship, you

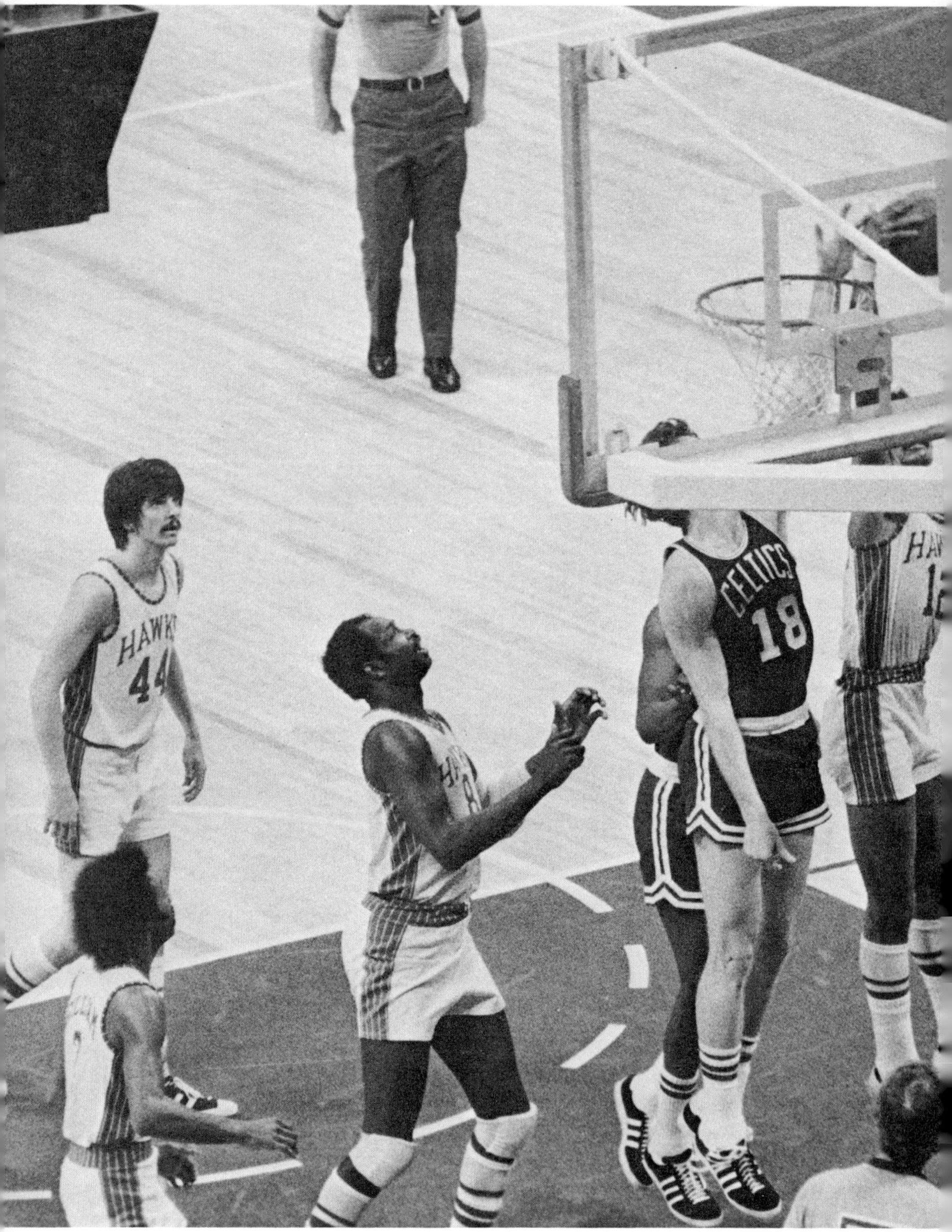
HAWKS
44
CELTICS
18

Jim Washington grabbing a defensive rebound during the 1972-73 playoffs against Boston with Pete getting ready to lead the break the other way.

want more. You think certain thoughts when you're going bad and other thoughts when you're going good."

But to this day Fitzsimmons denies that Pete's style of play led to his departure. "Pete fit into a 46-36 season in 1972-73, and I accepted that but I wasn't happy with our performance last season (36-46)," he admitted. "We didn't do the things I wanted, but I think it's very unfair to lay the blame for that on Pete's shoulders. He did what he's paid to do," also mentioning that the other Hawks did not do what they were paid to do.

The trade of Maravich did not raise too many eyebrows among his former teammates, although they certainly did not expect it.

"I'm never surprised by trades, since Wilt Chamberlain and Oscar Robertson were traded," says "Super" Lou Hudson, the other part of the high-scoring duo during Maravich's days with Atlanta. "I hate to see Pete go, because I think he has a tremendous amount of talent. But if the trade is going to make him happy, then that's good. We're in a game where it requires happiness to be able to do the job. And all of us in basketball are in a position to be traded. It should never be a big shock. One day it might come for me, if I stay in the game long enough."

Hudson, however, admitted, he did not think that Pete would ever be traded.

"I thought he would be here to close the shop after everybody else was gone. As far as sheer talent is concerned, not many have more than Pete. He is an exceptional ball handler and one of the better shooters in the game. Not because of his percentage, but because the shots he does take are tough ones. I have seen him make a tough move, and in the quick glimpse you get of his face then, you know he thinks he can make it. He has a very positive attitude."

Hudson, however, contradicted Fitzsimmons, saying that he felt that Maravich and Fitzsimmons did not hit it off. "I knew there was an aggravation on both parts. But Cotton and Pete never stopped talking to each other. There were no scenes in the dressing room or elsewhere. Still, I didn't think it would reach the point where they would trade him."

Another teammate, Herm Gilliam, Pete's backcourt partner, had already made plans for summer workouts with Maravich. "We were going to get started working in May," said Gilliam. "We were both disappointed about losing last year and wanted to do something about it. As a friend I can only wish Pete the best. I know the load he's been carrying, especially since the season ended the way it did. I think in the time we were together in Atlanta we had helped each other. I feel I learned something about offense from him, and he learned some defense from me."

And the reaction from Atlanta fans ran mostly in disapproval of the trade. One wrote: "We like the other players, but let's face it—Pete's talent was the drawing card. We, and many others we know, wouldn't have gone to any games if The Pistol hadn't been playing."

Another said: "As a three-year Hawk season ticket holder, I must voice my disgust with the latest blunder by Hawk management in the 'Pete Maravich Affair.' As a means of protest, I and many others will stay home next season. It doesn't take an expert to realize that the Hawks' lack of outstanding play at center over the past few years has prevented them from being an outstanding team. But somehow the Hawk management has refused to meet this problem head-on and instead has chosen to use Maravich as their scapegoat for losing."

In New Orleans the fans' reaction was that the price was possibly too high, but most admitted they were anxious to see the former LSU idol perform.

One wrote: "I can't believe it. That's way too much to pay for anybody. He's great and I can't wait to see him, but he won't have anybody to back him up."

Another said: "Out of all the players in the NBA, he's the most ideal for the New Orleans team. But the price was too high. Still if you want to get something good, you have to give up something good in return."

And that something good happens to be the top drawing attraction in the NBA, who has improved and honed his game ever since his controversial rookie year and up to his arrival as a bona fide superstar.

A Rembrandt

"The trade for Maravich was like getting a Rembrandt for a bunch of water colors," says Rosenfeld of the spectacular Pete, a much more modern artist, who has led the charge in altering the conventional NBA style of play to a more flamboyant one.

To this, Pete answers simply. "I am a fundamentalist."

Some fundamentalist. He certainly does not look the part and has been called a variety of things, including "showboat," "hot dog," and many other less complimentary names since the "Legend of Pete Maravich" began in earnest on the Baton Rouge campus of Louisiana State University.

But Pete has helped quiet the dissenters since his college days after his first two years as a pro. The change began during the 1972-73 season when he finished fifth in the league in scoring and sixth in assists. And less was heard after his final in Atlanta in which Pete closed as the runnerup to scoring champion Bob McAdoo of the Buffalo Braves with a 27.7 average.

The Pistol continued smoking all year with possibly the highlight of his career coming in a game in December of 1972. The Hawks were in Houston, again, (remember that was the scene of Pete's two-day suspension), and Maravich was suffering through a terrible shooting night for three quarters. Then with the Rockets leading by eight points as the fourth quarter began, Pete took aim.

With three minutes remaining to play, The Pistol unloaded

his arsenal, and it turned into the wild, wild west once again. First Pete knifed in for a layup and completed the three-point play after he was found. He then connected on a long 29-footer, and then, falling down, hit on a 21-footer. Another jumper from 20 feet followed, and Pete was at it again, breaking loose for a layup after a steak and then drilling in another 20-footer.

With 46 seconds remaining, Maravich unloaded again and hit a 17-foot basket to give the Hawks the lead at 122-121. Herm Gilliam fired in the Hawks' final three points, and Atlanta had a 125-123 victory.

In Maravich's uncanny spurt his deadly accuracy was good for 15 consecutive Hawks' points as he hit on 7-of-7 from the field and the lone free throw. His explosion took all of 2 minutes and 15 seconds, equalling his output for the rest of his evening's work as he finished with 30 points.

"My game is still explosive," said Maravich afterwards. "This was a time I knew there was no reason to hold back. I would've shot from 40 feet, and it would have gone in because I had my game going."

That was the Rembrandt Rosenfeld was speaking of.

Another time, late in December at the Omni, it is the Buffalo Braves and heralded $450,000 rookie-of-the-year Ernie DiGregorio providing the oppositon. DiGregorio, the former Providence great, is a slightly younger version of Maravich, complete with the behind-the-back passes and fancy dan moves.

And you know, The Pistol is well aware of this imposer, imposing on his territory. For although suffering from a painful heel injury, Pete played. Although played is an injustice to the word. Pete Maravich performed that night. He sparkled.

It was like a Fourth of July spectacular with The Pistol in all his resplendent glory. And when the debris had cleared, Pete had scored 42 points, passed off for an additional 10 assists, all in but 32 minutes of playing time.

On one play Pete intercepted an errant Buffalo pass, swept past DiGregorio with a behind-the-back dribble, then closed the curtain on his act by whipping a behind-the-back pass to teammate John Tschogl into an easy layup.

That is what Fitzsimmons meant when he stated, "Pete is the most exciting player in basketball. There is no player more explosive than he. If the score is close late in the game, I have

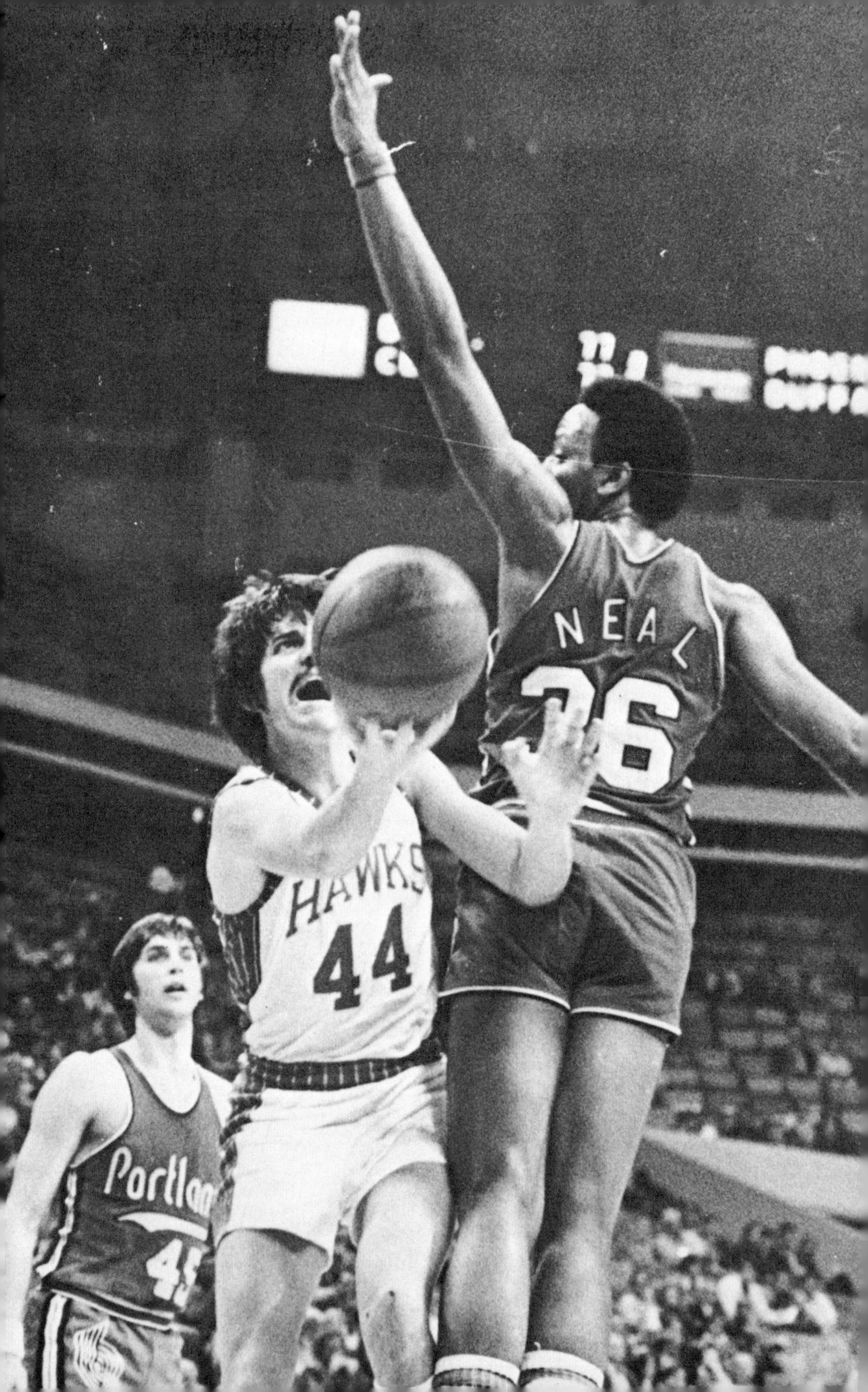
NEAL
26
HAWKS
44
Portland
45

Looking like a Rembrandt as he tosses in a driving layup against Portland. Geoff Petrie can only watch from behind in amazement.

complete confidence in his ability to score and bring us back."

Which brings us to the question of Maravich again. Rembrandt or hot dog?

"I don't like the word fancy," says Maravich of another word used often in describing his "showtime" on the court. "This denotes hot dogging it. I don't hot dog it. I describe it as deception. If you look one way and pass another, it gives you deception and a moment's advantage on the direction of the play. Individually, I'm a runner, and I do things on the run. This is my game."

Then Pete, the innovator, goes on to explain that the game is changing, and for the better. "The game itself is changing. In a few years I believe the chest pass will be obsolete just as the set shot is obsolete now. When I first started playing basketball, I used the set shot. Where is it now?"

Dead, Pete, dead. Right on.

"I'm doing the same things I did when I was three years old," he says. "This is my type of game. It will eventually revolutionize basketball. I'm already getting letters from coaches and parents, complaining about the tricky stuff. It's gonna be tough at first," he admits.

But it has always been tough for people to be different. Years ago long hair and beards were associated with weirdos. Now it is commonplace.

Pete's thoughts on basketball are the same. He feels that Bob Cousy, the Boston Celtic star of the 1950s and 1960s who brought to basketball the behind the back pass, started the changing trend in modern basketball.

"For me, it's different," says the serious Pete. "Bob Cousy did it sometimes, but I do it all the time. It's like when I'm driving for a basket," he adds. "Let's say I get around my man on the baseline. I can do that. Now there's a center waiting for me. Fine. That doesn't bother me. I'll drive on him. I look right at the man. I don't look where I'm going to pass. I hold the ball out to him—then I flick the ball off in any direction. Anywhere. I can do it. I've practiced this all my life. I have perfect

Pete fighting off a Bob Kauffman pick as he sticks tightly to Ernie DiGregorio in a 1973-74 regular season game against Buffalo.

Taking it on the chin, Henry Bibby of the New York Knicks.

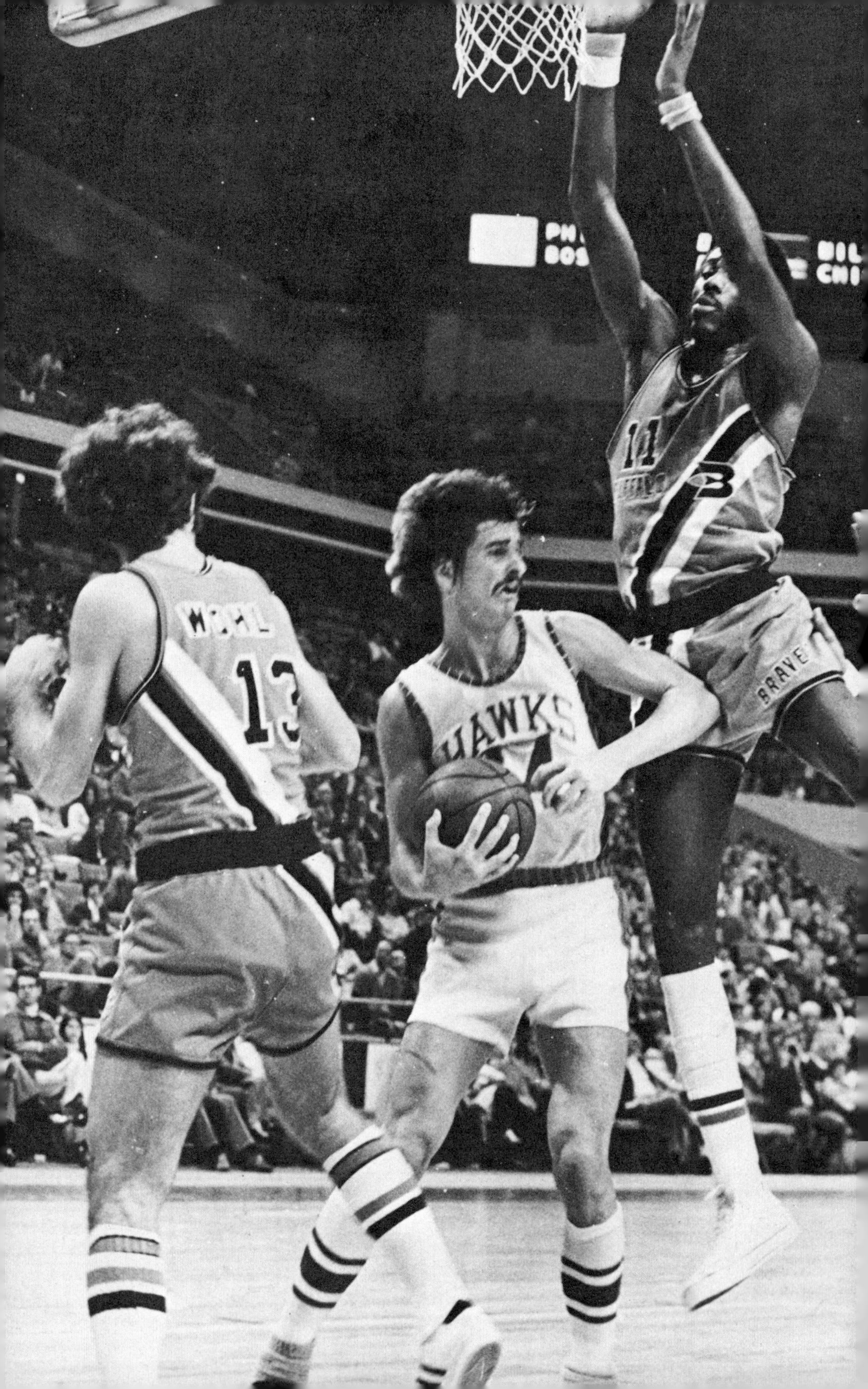
WOHL
13
HAWKS
11

control."

Rembrandt or fancy Dan, take your choice, but the fans come, and he is exciting, maybe even crazy, like that center Pete was talking about.

"See, I want that center to be thinking. 'Hey, man, this guy is crazy, he'll do anything.' Because once he starts thinking that," says Pete, "I've got him. I don't need to look at the ball. If you practice, you don't need to look at it. People have never looked into this. They just say, 'He's a hot dog.'

"Well, that's life. Fifty percent are for you. Fifty percent are against you. I don't mind that. But what bothers me is to think I didn't win somebody over because he didn't have the slightest idea what I was doing—or how much time I put in.

"I'm more specialized than a doctor or a lawyer. I've been doing this since I was three. People don't know that. That's what hurts me."

And Maravich's style of not doing the usual has had an influence on the NBA. Now there are many in the league who perform in the same manner as Maravich, although not quite as majestically.

But Maravich does not perform his sleight of hand magic at random. He makes the percentage pass and saves "showtime" until a game is safely tucked away in the win column.

Skip Caray, the voice of the Hawks, who has watched Maravich's career in Atlanta, notes a change in Pete. "He has matured," says Caray. "As I have always said, the only person who could stop Pete Maravich is Maravich himself. If he has one fault, it's that he has so much confidence in his ability that when a play fails he will return to it until it succeeds."

A Rembrandt or a hot dog? How about perfectionist.

"To me, basketball is almost like an art form," says Maravich, speaking more like Rembrandt. "Not that my game will revolutionize basketball, but my style will influence a gradual evolution."

Pete foresees the giants of the game, 6-foot-8 players whipping passes behind their backs, just as he does now.

"An act of deception," is the way Pete describes it.

Pete taking a rebound away from Buffalo's Bob McAdoo, the NBA's leading scorer in 1973-74.

"That's what this game is all about. A series of acts of deception. But each one has to have a purpose, it's got to be meaningful. Like if I'm on a two-on-one fast break, if I look to my teammate and pass to him every time, there's no deception.

"My pass would be intercepted eight times out of ten. But if I fake a pass behind my back, keep the ball and shoot—or pass behind my back, that's deception. That creates baskets," says the game's topnotch showman.

"Other times I throw a simple straightaway chest pass, but that's deception, too. The guy guarding me isn't expecting it. He doesn't know what to expect from me. He's more concerned about a flashy pass. And when I throw a simple basic pass, he's not ready for it. He's expecting something else so the chest pass goes right by him. In that situation a chest pass is just as much an act of deception as a flashy pass. It's all got to have a purpose."

In all his masterful ploys of deception has Pete ever noticed his defender's startled face?

"Not really," says Pete, "because to see his face, I'd have to look back. Going by somebody, I've never looked back."

Looking Back

Pete may never look back, but in examining his emergence as a superstar in the NBA you have to look back—to the 1972-73 season. That is when Pete arrived with all the frills, among the cream of the NBA crop. It was also the season in which the Hawks had a new coach in Cotton Fitzsimmons and a new building to play in, the Omni, a magnificent structure which seats 16,500 for basketball.

In his new setting, after playing the first two years at Georgia Tech's ancient Alexander Memorial Coliseum, with a seating capacity of 7,000, Pete finally arrived after a fantastic three-year career at LSU and a pair of streaky years as a pro.

That was the year that opponents stopped pounding him and stopped laughing and sneering at his sometimes wild, unorthodox passes. Instead they voted him to start in the NBA All-Star game.

In the game, playing for the East Stars in Chicago on January 23rd, Pete saw 22 minutes of action and tossed in eight points in a winning effort. All the little refinements were beginning to show now in Pete's game. He was also a little older and more mature, although still a showman.

"I really don't use the flashy stuff too much any more. I got tired of hearing how Pete Maravich was just a hot dog, so I stick pretty much to straight basketball now," he said.

Do not believe a word of it though. A good example of it was during the All-Star break. During a practice session he jokingly told his teammates: "Okay guys, I'm gonna give a little

That is Pete behind the ball, doing his famous "spinning the ball on his finger" act.

clinic," grinning his famous mischievous smile. He then proceeded to spring into his routine of tricky moves, gaining the laughter of the squad and even getting some of them to join in the fun.

He was again the master showman—doing his thing, first he was spinning a basketball on his index finger, then tossing the ball between his legs. He climaxed his act by switching the rotating ball to his left hand, flipping it into the air, and then knocking it soccer-style, with his head, into the basket.

But in the game itself he played it straight—almost. He only threw four or five behind-the-back passes and waltzed in for a pair of tantalizing drives past West center Wilt Chamberlain for two-pointers.

"Hey, big guy," Maravich shouted to Chamberlain after the game. "Don't get mad at me for those drives. Somebody told me your full extension is 12 feet, 9 inches, so I've been working on a 12 feet, 10 inch arc on my shots."

And it was during this break that Fitzsimmons said of Maravich: "He's playing the best all-around game of his career. Maybe he's not quite as flashy as he used to be, but I find him delightful to watch. It's very enjoyable to me to see him playing some defense, even if that doesn't excite the crowds."

But it was something that Maravich was working on.

"I guess anybody can play defense if he concentrates," said Maravich. "I know I still have a long way to go to be considered a real good defensive player, but I'm working at it. I've decided to let the offensive and scoring come naturally, and I'm thinking more about playing defense.

"I know we're gonna get a lot of points, and I'm gonna get my share of them," he said. "I don't have to think about doing that. I want to be a better ballplayer, and that means I have to play defense and be a little more controlled on offense."

The bout with Bell's Palsy was a thing of the past, and it showed in Pete's performance up to the All-Star game.

"I weighed over 200 pounds for the first time in my life at the start of the season," said Maravich. "I had regained all of my strength and weight I had lost from having mono, and I felt better than ever. The Bell's Palsy messed me up a little, but I still feel stronger than I usually do this late in the season."

But the season had started on a near tragic note, and even

Pete and Lou Hudson sharing the trophy as Co-Most Valuable Players on the Hawks after the 1972-73 season.

Pete had his doubts that he would even be playing basketball again, let alone being a member of the All-Star squad. It all began one afternoon early in November in a hotel room on the road when he was washing his face before going out to dinner. He gazed into the mirror and saw one of his eyes was half closed. Then he noticed his cheek and mouth muscles sagging. And worst of all, he had absolutely no control over any of it!

Pete's health problems had begun about a week earlier when he awakened with a headache for five straight days. He visited a doctor who prescribed medication and was told he would be all right in a few days.

Although playing with the painful headaches, Maravich was sharing his pain with his opponents, first scoring 31 points against Houston and then pouring in 44 against Philadelphia as the Hawks won both games. At that point in the early going the Hawks had a 6-6 record, and Maravich was third in the league in scoring with a 26.4 average.

Then the illness was finally diagnosed. It was Bell's Palsy, a rare disease described by doctors as a disturbance of the nerve that controls facial muscles on one side of the face. Doctors said they did not know what caused it but said it should go away within a couple of weeks—or a couple of years.

"I figured it would be two or three years," says Pete. "I went up to my room and cried."

His teammates tried to make it easier on the worried Pete, kidding him, and calling him "Half Face." They made him laugh when he wanted to cry and showed compassion by sticking with him, letting him know he was not alone in his time of crisis.

Physicians had no solution for the ailment except to instruct Pete to continually massage the facial muscles and avoid drafts. So Pete would sit for hours, rubbing his face in corners, away from windows and air conditioning units. "It was a horrible feeling," Pete remembers. "It really freaked me out."

To say Pete was worried was an understatement. He was scared, and no one could blame him one bit. Last year it had been mononucleosis and now this, an affliction that had previously hit other star athletes like ex-football star John David Crow and former baseball great Roger Maris.

Fitzsimmons said he thought it was "more of a mental thing. Pete's got in the back of his mind the fact that something physical seems to have happened to him ever since coming into the pros. He's the type of dedicated athlete who builds up nervous energy. And this is something you can't store in either the mind or the body. So the big thing he has to do now is get himself mentally ready to play," said his coach.

"Pete wants to play," said Fitzsimmons. "He was excused from practice, but he came anyway. There is no danger in Pete playing, unless the eye is injured. And I don't want him playing in goggles."

Playing with specially-made glasses to protect his eye in the Hawks' previous game, Maravich could only play six

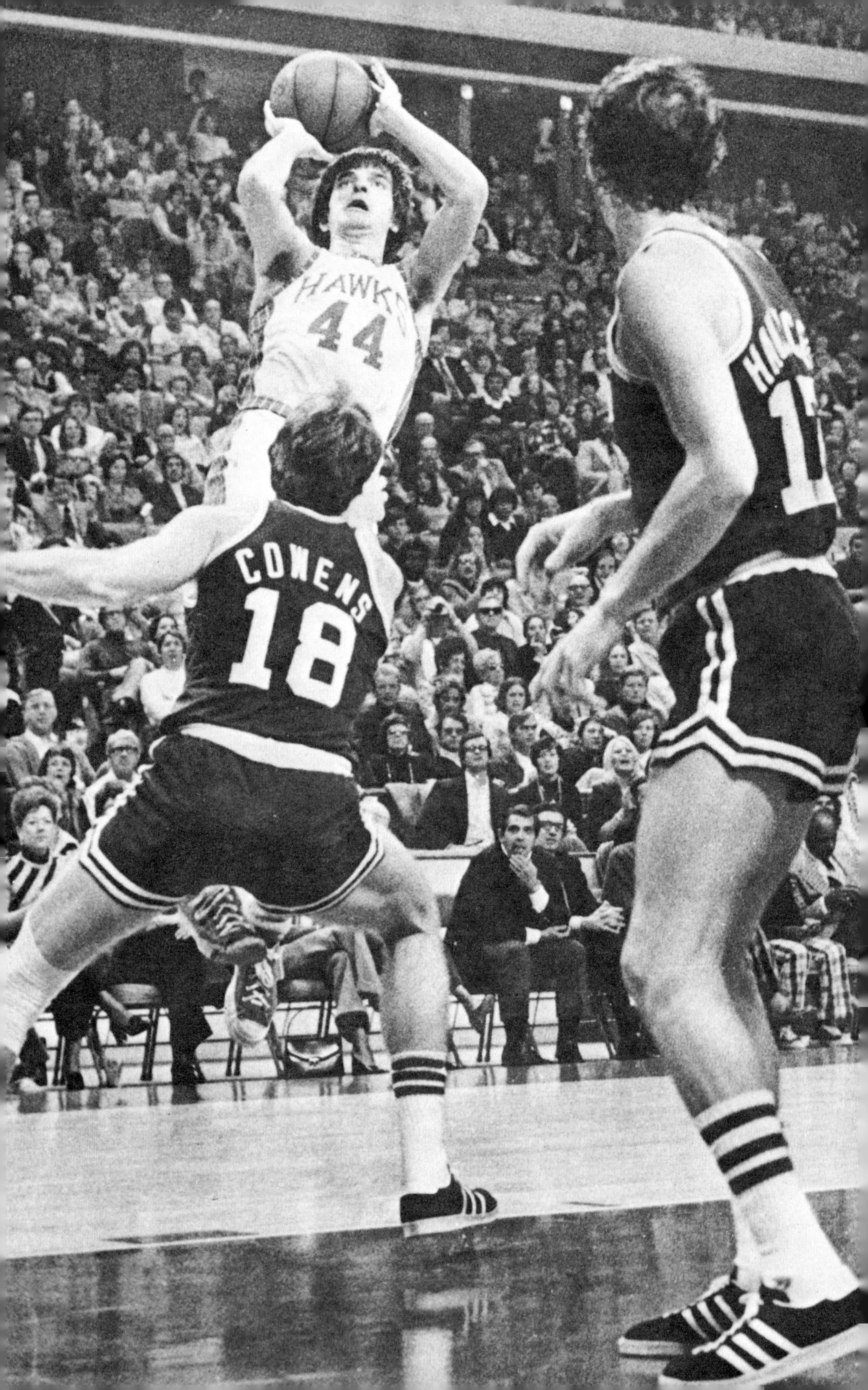
HAWKS
44
COWENS
18

minutes and failed to score a point. His scoring average dropped from 26.3 to 24.5 points per game.

But Maravich was not worried about his statistics. His affliction was his only concern. He still could not close his right eye, making it dangerous to play since he could not protect the eye against a poke in it by an errant finger.

Fortunately, however, in less than three weeks the ailment disappeared, and Pete was his normal self again. The doctors told him the palsy might never return, although he was somewhat more prone to get it than someone who had never had it, the doctors said.

Asked if the palsy could have been an aftermath of Maravich's bout with mononucleosis a year before, General Manager Richie Guerin said there was no association whatsoever.

Then it was thought that it may have occurred due to an eye injury Pete suffered in a preseason game, but Guerin dismissed it, saying, "No. That injury occurred in a scrimmage when Pete got an elbow in the eye, and, as I remember it, it took five or six stitches to close the cut.

"The eye never bothered him, and he was off to an excellent start this season," said Guerin. "He cut down on his turnovers and was playing good D (defense), but he's a highly emotional young man.

"I don't know what emotions have anything to do with it, but Pete is a young man who always has put too much pressure on himself. At any rate, the slight paralysis has responded to medication and treatment. It's like a virus."

Although he tried playing with the goggles, to no avail, Maravich said he was going to play even though the condition prevented him from closing his right eye. "I can't sit around forever," he said. "There's some pain behind the neck and around the ears, and I have to wear a patch or tape the eye shut to sleep. It's been driving me crazy." So he went back to driving the rest of the NBA crazy, and it soon wore off, and he could sleep and play once again with the weird twitch in his eye.

Pete's full recovery showed by season's end when his

Pete hitting for 2 of his 37 points in the third game of the 1972-73 playoffs against Boston.

statistics showed him with 2,063 points and 546 assists. He and Herm Gilliam were the only teammates in the league to finish in the Top Ten in assists, and he and Lou Hudson, who scored 2,029 points, were only the second teammate pair to score more than 2,000 points in one season in the history of the NBA. Jerry West and Elgin Baylor of Los Angeles had previously accomplished the feat during the 1964-65 season.

Capping his excellent season Pete was named to the ten-man NBA All-Star squad. He had arrived.

And so had the Hawks, reversing their record of the previous season and finishing with a 46-36 record and fighting into a playoff spot against the Boston Celtics.

Boston won the series four games to two, but in Game No. 4, with the Celtics holding a 2-1 advantage, Maravich had his finest post-season effort. On that pleasant Sunday afternoon in Atlanta Pete scored 37 points, having five assists and seven rebounds in the 97-94 victory.

"I thought he played a whale of a game," said Coach Fitzsimmons. "He ran the club. He had a couple of bad spurts, got a little wild, but down the stretch I thought he also did a good job of defense on Havlicek."

John Havlicek, Boston's version of baseball's Pete Rose, had gotten 21 points to lead the Celtics. But that was well below his series average after throwing in a remarkable 54 points in the opening victory in Boston, 29 in the Celtics second game triumph, and 18 in Game No. 3.

In the fourth quarter the Celtics switched to a Havlicek-Maravich matchup, and The Pistol responded with a fine defensive effort. He also scored 13 of Atlanta's final 20 points. "Pete hit some tough shots," said Havlicek afterward.

Two games later it was all over as the Hawks were eliminated 121-103 as Pete scored only 12 points, hitting on but six of twenty-one shots from the field.

"Pete was ready to play," said Fitzsimmons. "He was doing the best he could do. The guys in the green suits (Boston) knew how they had to play him."

But that was only one of the rare "off nights" for Pete in his finest season as Houston guard Mike Newlin will testify.

After Maravich had scored 35 points in a game with the Rockets just prior to the playoffs, Newlin said he felt that

Maravich drives against No. 14 Mike Newlin of Houston, who states that Pete is his toughest defensive assignment.

Maravich had arrived as a superstar. "Two players give me a lot of trouble in this league," said Newlin, a fine guard and one of the top defenders in the league. "Maravich and Nate Archibald. But Pete is the toughest. His biggest asset is his quickness. He is more of a total player than Nate. I played one of my best games defensively and he still scored 35. I played as tough a defense as it is possible to play."

Newlin added that Pete was "open a lot more times and didn't get the ball. I sincerely consider him an unselfish player. I know he looks to make the pass to an open teammate more than they look for him.

"Maravich is the reason Atlanta is a winner," said Newlin.

"Atlanta's development can be traced to the way Pete developed."

Prior to the season, the Hawks felt that a strong forward could possibly insure an NBA title so they decided to raid the rival American Basketball Association. They chose to sign Julius Erving, better known as Doctor J, one of the ABA's top stars. But after a lengthy squabble in the courts and out, Irving was declared a Virginia Squire and went back to the ABA after practicing with the Hawks in preseason camp. And to this day Erving recalls the way Pete Maravich always had the ball in the right place for him on the fast break. But no one will ever know what the trio of Lou Hudson, Erving, and Maravich could have done together.

So the Hawks had to come up with something else in place of Erving. That something was to leave Maravich alone, according to the plan of Cotton Fitzsimmons, the new coach who had never had a losing season anywhere, including two years with the NBA Phoenix Suns.

"When I coached against Pete Maravich, he didn't hurt us every night," said Cotton. "He was inconsistent. I didn't know what to expect."

Fitzsimmons had also heard that Pete was an individualist but decided to leave him alone. He knew that Pete had only one coach in his life—his father Press.

"Press Maravich put in all that time, taught Pete the game," said Cotton. "And I wasn't going to change him. I hope some day Pete will think I'm a good coach. But he'll always think Press is the greatest."

All he did was give the Hawks the ball and tell them to run and it paid off.

"I've got to run," says Pete. "If I don't run, I'm pitiful."

The season started out with Maravich and Hudson at the guard spots, Jimmy Washington and George Trapp at forward, and Walt Bellamy at center. After a 10-13 slate, Cotton made the change that produced the fine season. He moved Hudson, an agile 6-foot-5, who could go at either forward or guard, back to the front court and inserted Herm Gilliam into the starting lineup as the guard to team with Maravich.

The switch loosened up the Hawks. Pete, somewhat of a loner his first two years, began to come out from his shell with

Gilliam and Washington doing the prodding. And the team began to win.

When the season ended, Pete proved that he does two things better than anyone in the league—handle the ball and shoot on the move.

"I was criticized for everything I did when I came into the league," says Pete. "I believe if people keep criticizing enough, you'll finally do something that'll justify their criticism. I admit I make mistakes, but the mistakes were blown out of proportion because that's what everyone was looking for. They kept harping, 'Why do you dribble into traffic?' I enjoy going into traffic, that's my game. I can create that way. That's what me and a lot of young guys are into—revolutionizing basketball."

He was also criticized by players on opposing teams. And Pete did not help the situation any by putting his act into high gear by going with a between-the-legs dribble or an off-the-ear layup.

"They should know I wasn't doing this to embarrass or hot dog," says Pete. "It's my art. It's my deception. But you're talking about envy and jealousy."

He was referring to his huge contract which was just pure professional hatred—it was the poor boy against the noveau riche, the traditional against the innovative.

"It doesn't bother me," says Pete. "I'm just trying to do a job."

And he sees his job as entertainment.

"That fan is paying $5-$7-$10-$12 a ticket. He's entitled to something for his money," Pete says. "He could go out and buy a dinner and a movie for the price he pays for a ticket. He should get total satisfaction from watching a game."

"Showtime" has made Maravich the No. 1 NBA attraction and one of the most recognizable pro athletes in the country.

Like the time in Kansas City, a farmer climbed aboard a bus the Hawks were in, and says: "I don't mean any harm, but I've watched professional basketball on television and I like to recognize the players. Which one is Pete Maverick?" he says.

Herm Gilliam laughed, then said: "That's Pete Maverick over there," pointing to Pete. The farmer then said hello and left.

Another time it is Milwaukee, and an usher says, "You can tell Maravich is playing here today. All the teenyboppers are here."

Maravich is no longer young and unsophisticated as he was when he left LSU. The attention and adulation is still there. But Pete still does not crave it and works hard to keep it from separating him from his teammates.

But as flamboyant as he is on the court, Maravich is just the opposite in private life.

"I enjoy being alone," he says. "After all the travel and excitement of the games, it is good to be alone and think.

"I like to do some of my own cooking. On the road we eat in restaurants, and I see enough of them, so when I'm home I stick around the place. Now I'm no gourmet...I just cook simple stuff like steak."

And although he can be seen joking and whispering comfortably with his teammates, he does not like to talk about his personal life.

"I guard my privacy like an African chieftain guards his village," he says. "I'm kind of a recluse. I don't like people making a fuss over me. It's hard for me to go out. When I'm going out to dinner I go when everybody else is coming home from work. The restaurants are empty, and that's how I like it. I like to eat alone.

"One thing I don't do is sign an autograph when I'm eating. I'll spend any amount of time signing autographs, and I've signed millions. But not when I'm eating. That's an invasion of privacy, and I wouldn't do that to anyone. Before I eat, that's okay, or after I'm finished, that's okay too. Otherwise, forget it."

Maravich is still one of sport's most eligible bachelors, but unlike a Joe Namath, he refuses to talk about his girlfriends.

"I've got to keep some part of my life for myself," he says. "My weight drops from 207 to 185 during the season. There's all those injuries, needles, rehabilitation. I need those three to four months to get my head together. I don't want to talk about my off-season. That's mine.

"That's one part of my life the public will never know about. I will not expose my private life to anybody. I spend it with people I like to spend my time with."

In Atlanta he also came under criticism for his unavailability to writers after games.

"There were times that I just didn't want to talk," explains Pete. "Especially after a loss. And there were other times that a writer would ask me to comment on a teammate. What they were trying to do was get me to knock my teammates. Put words in my mouth. So I figured the best thing to do was to say nothing at all.

"Basketball is an emotional game, and you're still emotional after the games. So I think that is the time to cool off, not pop off."

What Pete is saying is that he should be judged by what he does on the basketball court, and that should be enough.

"I'm not pleased with anything I've done so far," he says of his exploits on the court. "There's so much more to do. I've won scoring titles and I've got lots of money, but that doesn't mean anything.

"All I want to do is win the title. A title would be the highest level you can attain. They'll say, 'He was a hot dog—but he was a champion.' I could care less about the money. I could be a beach bum. I could survive."

But you wonder if this man who puts his soul on the line each time he is out on the floor could survive.

You have to wonder, when he says: "The best time is late in the game. You're up by six or eight points. Then all of a sudden we do a few things. I dish out three or four assists. I make some move they've never seen before. We run them off the court. Up in the stands people are dropping popcorn on their heads. They can't believe it. Then the game is over, and we've won. The fans don't want to leave. That's what really turns me on."

Although he was to be an All-Star after but three years in the league, his development was apparently not quick enough for his detractors who expected him to be an instant superstar after his triumphant career at LSU. It seemed like all of Atlanta was waiting to be turned on by the kid from Aliquippa, Pennsylvania, waiting for him to finally bring "showtime" to the South in his sophomore season in the NBA.

Pete's Second Year, 1971-1972

But the 1971-72 season started on a dismal note, with initially, Hawks coach Richie Guerin missing the opening two days of training camp with a kidney infection, and then Pete contracting mononucleosis, although it took weeks to finally diagnose his illness.

Then began a series of trades in the youth movement. It was to be the beginning of the Pete Maravich Era in Atlanta. After the dust had settled, the only Hawk remaining of the ones who came from St. Louis only two years before when the franchise shifted to Atlanta, was "Super" Lou Hudson.

Gone were Walt Hazzard and Jerry Chambers, sent off to Buffalo for Donnie May and Herm Gilliam. Then Jimmy Davis and John Vallely were shipped to Houston for Don Adams and Larry Siegfried. And finally it was captain Bill Bridges, going to Philadelphia for Jim Washington.

The absence of Maravich, whose gaunt, haunting shadow was missing from the hardwood for 14 games with mono, was ruled the downfall of the Hawks that season. However, Atlanta, although suffering with a 36-46 record, did make it into the playoffs.

The primary reason for the poor record, however, was not dissension, as some thought, but that the team just did not know each other, what with all the trades and learning each other's moves.

"How in the world can there be dissension," said Hudson, "when you hardly know the guy dressing next to you. We don't know each other well enough yet to argue."

Which was true. Of the team that finished the season, only seven were there at the beginning. It was not until the close of the campaign that the Hawks started to jell, capturing eight of their last ten games.

There were some highlights of the season such as Maravich's two 50-point performances; Walt Bellamy's 18 first half rebounds against Seattle; Hudson's many 41-point efforts; and Herm Gilliam's career high 30 points against Cleveland.

But they were offset by many low points which included the rumors that Richie Guerin would be replaced as coach—which he ultimately was, although remaining as general manager; Pete taking only one shot in a game against Seattle, and missing it; and the season itself.

It finally ended in the playoffs with the Boston Celtics taking the best-of-seven series, four games to two.

The season had opened on the wrong foot at training camp in Jacksonville, Florida, when in the second week Maravich was kicked in the calf and missed a couple of days. Walt Bellamy had to spend a week in the hospital with the flu, and Lou Hudson came down with a back ailment.

Then the illnesses really got serious as Maravich checked into a Jacksonville hospital on September 15 for five days of tests. Doctors at first diagnosed his problem as an infection of the tonsils, then thought it was strep throat. His temperature soared to 103, and now scarlet fever was feared. And so he remained in the hospital until the temperature came back down to normal.

Finally on October 4 it was diagnosed in Atlanta as infectious mononucleosis, and Pete would miss the opening 14 games of the regular season, plus the rest of training camp. His weight dropped from 205 pounds to 169, and he would not be an effective part of the Hawks until mid-December.

It was a crushing blow to the multi-talented Maravich, who had a rocky introduction to the pro game as a rookie but had finally established himself as the quarterback of the club in the early days of training camp.

Pete was finally released from the hospital after a week but was told to rest at his apartment with his only exercise restricted to walking. "I hope to be running at full speed by the first week in November," said the optimistic Pete. But it was to be another month before he was restored to the starting lineup.

Pete recalls the experience with a smile now, but it certainly was not funny at the time, especially that last day in the Jacksonville hospital.

"I was determined to get out of that place," he says, "so I arranged the night before for a seat on a flight to Atlanta. The next morning I broke out in a rash. I mean the darndest rash you ever saw. I also had a fever of 103 degrees.

"When the doctor came by for the morning checkup, I

Maravich being guarded by Houston's Calvin Murphy.

Pete taking a rebound during the 1972-73 playoffs against Boston. That is center Dave Cowens of the Celtics watching.

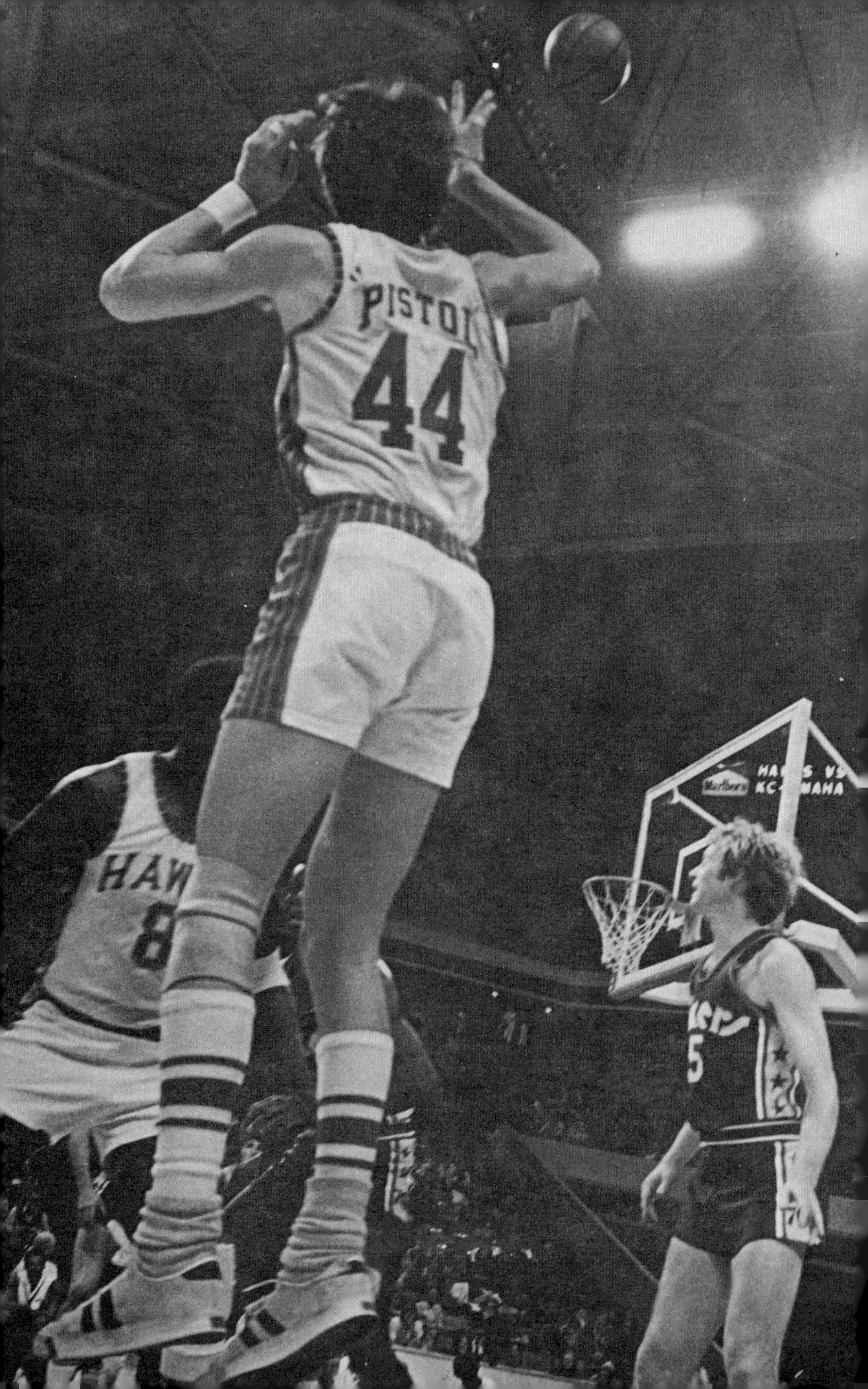
PISTOL
44
HAW
8

told him I was leaving. And when he said, 'You mean, you won't stay?' I replied, 'No, I'm going.'

"That's when he said, 'I think you have scarlet fever.' And I answered, 'Well, if I'm going to die, I want to die in Atlanta.'"

Pete's throat infection had been so painful that he recalls, "I was in such pain I couldn't even talk. I had to write out messages on a clipboard to the nurses."

He still did not know how long he would be out of action, saying, "I don't know how long it will take me to get my timing back because I've never had any extended injury or illness before."

Late in October, two weeks after leaving the hospital, Maravich worked out briefly, shooting a few baskets and running around the court ten times. "I thought I was going to black out," says Pete. "Not being able to play is the worst feeling in the world. I'm awfully weak. I'll be back as soon as possible, but there's no way to tell when."

It was to be another five weeks before Pete returned, but the illness had sapped his strength and left him physically weak. However, he finished the year remarkably with a 19.3 per game scoring average, with 1,275 points in 66 games, and increasing his assists output from his rookie season by 38 to 393. And in the playoff loss to Boston The Pistol gunned for a 27.7 average and nearly five assists a game.

At the midway point in the campaign, after gradually regaining some pounds on his already thin frame, Maravich tossed in his pro career-high 50 points in a 124-116 victory over Philadelphia and even won the right to play in the NBA's One-On-One Contest, defeating his teammates for the right to represent the Hawks. He called that contest the "most draining type of basketball you can play," claiming that the competition within the Hawks had left him worn out "for a week."

After his bout with mono which saw his weight go down 34 pounds, to a low of 169, he gradually gained some of it back to 185 pounds.

"I won't be able to gain back much more of the weight

Bombs away against the Philadelphia 76ers, the team in which he scored his NBA career-high 50 points during the 1971-72 season.

this season," he explained. "It's frustrating because of the type of schedule we play. Some nights I can't move at all because I just don't have the stamina."

Pete said the three weeks he spent in the hospitals did not hurt his shooting but said that first real workout before coming back to play was brutal.

"I felt so frail out on the court," said Pete. "I thought to myself that I probably wouldn't be back in any kind of shape for the rest of the year. I shot for about 30 minutes and was completely worn out. I could hardly get back to my apartment."

The statistics did not show it, but perhaps the season was in many ways much better than his rookie year, at least mentally.

You have to wonder how this highly sensitive young man could have survived that year, when even his own teammates were hostile to the million-dollar man from the Bayou.

Pete Signs With The Hawks

The Pistol era in Atlanta began on March 23, 1970, when the Hawks made their first draft selection official, choosing the LSU scoring machine. But there was still no guarantee that Maravich would do his playing in Atlanta. The stakes were high, and the Carolina Cougars of the rival American Basketball Association were also after the services of the high-scoring Pete whose scoring abilities had the whole nation talking about him.

And so the bidding began. It was to resemble a high-stakes poker game between Hawks owner Tom Cousins, who had made his fortune in the construction business, and the equally youthful and wealthy Jim Gardner of the Cougars.

After the drafting of Pete, Cousins said: "I don't guess I should be sending Pete a message. But I intend to make it more pleasant for him to play in Atlanta than in Charlotte, Greensboro, or Raleigh."

Cousins was referring to the sites in which the Carolina franchise played its home games.

"I'm not afraid to compete with Carolina for him. And with everything else equal, I think Pete would rather play against the better competition in the NBA."

The question of how much money it would take to lure the kid who scored 50 points in his first outing as a college freshman four years before, came up.

"I can't answer that now," said Cousins. "In the first place it's not that definite yet. There are financial considerations plus various fringe benefits that I don't know how to put a pencil on."

And from the ABA came the warning of a frenzied bidding war for Pete's services.

"In the beginning the Cougars were awfully confident they would get Maravich," said a high ABA source. "Pete told them that he wouldn't play in San Diego and that he didn't like Detroit. Those were the teams the Cougars thought they were competing with," he said. "Then Atlanta entered the picture, and now the thinking up here (in Carolina) was that it is a whole new ball game. Now it boils down to a poker game, one with awfully high stakes, and who's got the most guts. That last word is spelled m-o-n-e-y."

And how right he was.

The Hawks had acquired the rights to bid for Maravich in the draft on January 29 when they obtained San Francisco's (now Golden State) No. 1 draft choice in exchange for the rights to center Zelmo Beaty, who had jumped to the ABA in 1969. The maneuver allowed the Hawks to draft third since the Warriors finished with the third worst record in the NBA during the 1969-70 campaign.

And so the battle for Maravich's signature began in earnest now.

The older league held a secret meeting and decided that Atlanta would get Maravich in the draft since Detroit, with the first choice, would go for Bob Lanier of St. Bonaventure, and San Diego, choosing second, would take Rudy Tomjanovich, a big forward from Michigan.

Asked if the league was prepared to back him in a dollars fight with Gardner and the ABA, Cousins answered, "Absolutely not. It's my baby all the way."

It was also learned that Gardner had asked the other ABA teams to give him a percentage of their gate receipts when and if Maravich plays with the Cougars.

As for Maravich's lawyers, they were also making plans.

"Our plans are to ask both Atlanta and Carolina to submit their proposals," said Arthur Herskowitz from Pete's hometown in Aliquippa, Pennsylvania. "We are hopeful, in fact, it will be within the next few days." Herskowitz then added that "Our staff will evaluate both offers and then advise Pete accordingly. The final decision, however, will be his. We will only point out the advantages and disadvantages of both offers and let him decide for himself."

"I don't know what it's going to take to get him, but we're going to make a big effort," said Atlanta coach Richie Guerin.

"I believe we can sign him," he said, leaving little doubt that it would be "showtime" whenever the explosive Maravich plays in Atlanta.

"I wouldn't want to change his style," said Guerin. "I'd want him to do his thing, with one change. He wouldn't shoot as much."

How about his droopy socks, do they come with the package?

"Listen," grinned Guerin. "He can wear bunting shoes if he comes to play. I can't think of any player drafted that would

Hawks owner Tom Cousins, Pete, and Poppa Press Maravich at the signing of "The Pistol's" $1.9 million contract on March 23, 1970.

have the impact on any city in the nation," said Guerin, "that Maravich will have on Atlanta.

"If we get him, we'll have some sort of attraction. There's no more exciting team right now than ours with Caldwell, Hudson, Hazzard, Bellamy, Bridges, and the rest. Add Maravich and this would be one helluva exciting outfit. And remember, what's good for Atlanta is good for the Hawks."

Three days later it was official, Pete Maravich was a Hawk. The brilliant basketball magician who says he's "always out to entertain," signed a five-year contract with the Hawks calling for $1.9 million.

"I wanted to play somewhere in the South," said Maravich at an elaborate press conference set up at one of Atlanta's posh hotels.

Richie Guerin, Pete's first pro coach.

Carolina was also located in the South, but Maravich reportedly turned down a $2 million offer from the Cougars and Gardner.

Pete's father Press sat beside his son along with Les Zittrain, one of the two attorneys who handled all the negotiations for the 1970 College Player of the Year, when the signing was announced.

It turned Maravich instantly into the highest paid amateur ever turning professional in sports history. But, at the time, no one wanted to discuss the exact terms of the contract.

"Let's just say it's a contract that is fair, one that handsomely compensates the greatest basketball player in the world," said Zittrain.

"I'm getting $85 a week," joked Pistol Pete. "I'm getting a pick, a shovel, and a tractor."

Press was asked how it felt to see his son sign such a huge contract?

"Who said it was big," replied the elder Maravich, who had taken up basketball as a youngster and had never made more than $4,500 a year in his pro career, after escaping from the coal mines of Pennsylvania. "I think it's going to be a good thing for Pete and for Atlanta," he said.

"Maybe I'm a little kookie," explained the 20-year-old Maravich, "but I'm always going to be out to entertain," he said of his planned pro career. "There's nothing that says you can't win and be entertaining."

But as he said then for the first time, and constantly repeats: "I don't want to be Pete Maravich 12 months a year. One of the happiest times I've had recently was when I went to Daytona Beach, sat on the sand, and nobody recognized me."

Although the bidding war was at a fever pitch between the rival leagues, it was over for the Hawks and Pete Maravich. Only a day earlier the Detroit Pistons of the NBA shelled out $1.6 million for Lanier, the 6-foot-11 giant all-American from St. Bonaventure in upstate New York. At the time of his signing, his pact eclipsed the $1.4 million Lew Alcindor (now Kareem Abdul Jabbar) received a year earlier for signing with the Milwaukee Bucks.

But Maravich's contract was even higher, equalling the same figure given to Spencer Haywood, who renegotiated his

Pete on one of his famed layups, challenging the center—this time it is Rick Roberson, then of Cleveland, showing why Atlanta went all out to sign him.

contract a day earlier with the Denver Rockets of the ABA. However, Haywood's money was to be paid out over six years, not the five years which Maravich's would be spread out.

But the big headline grabber was Maravich, the three-time all-American who led the nation in scoring three times with a lofty 44.2 scoring average and was holder of 11 NCAA records and 16 Southeastern Conference marks.

"This is the thing I've looked forward to," said Maravich at the signing. "It's like starting out as a freshman again. I wanted to play somewhere in the South, and I'm overly excited about playing in Atlanta."

Before the signing, Gardner of the rival ABA Cougars had threatened to raid Atlanta's roster if Maravich signed with the Hawks, but afterwards relented: "There are too many other good players around to be worried about one player."

Cousins, on the other hand, was excited, saying, "I hope it will be printed what great guys they are. Not only am I referring to the Maravich family, Press and Pete, but I also mean the two lawyers we had to deal with, Arthur Herskowitz and Les Zittrain."

Harmony was the keynote of that momentous day, but the troubles would lie ahead in the upcoming season for the rich rookie and the veteran Hawks.

But at the time, Cousins said, "I have talked with our players, and they said they think Pete is going to be great. But Pete is going to have to be awfully good not to be the highest paid substitute in the game."

Team captain Bill Bridges said, "It all worked out very fine. We are very fortunate."

Yet it was apparent that Bridges and some of the other Hawks, including Coach Richie Guerin, did not think Pete Maravich's arrival was the rosy picture everyone was painting.

The Summer Of Waiting

Two months had passed since Pete signed his historic contract with the Hawks, and it was still weeks away from the rookie camp in which he would make his pro debut. During the lull Pete was asked if he had any regrets on signing with the Hawks, rather than the Cougars or Globetrotters.

"None whatsoever," he said. "In fact, I'm delighted to have had the opportunity to sign with such an excellent organization. It is a solid club, and I believe Atlanta is potentially an exciting city for professional basketball."

Pete said he did not think his life had changed any since signing and would have to work hard on his game as a pro.

"I realize the tough challenges that lie ahead. I'm just going to polish up my whole game. I want to do what is best for the Hawk team. My goal is to help the Hawks, its organization, and fans, to win the NBA world championship.

"I don't expect my teammates to resent me because of my contract," said Pete, although that statement in part would be proven wrong. "Everyone has his own thing, and if any of the players make a zillion dollars, that's their business. Money doesn't have anything to do with the team, players, or character of the players. My dad has always taught me to respect ability, character, and integrity in an individual."

Maravich said he probably felt like any other rookie entering a pro career.

"I am no different," he said. "I'll work hard. Ever since I was a little boy I've dreamed of playing professional basketball.

Pete pondering a question at a press conference, something he had to do many times after his historic signing with the Hawks.

I realize the road ahead will be bumpy, but if I work hard it will become smoother. It will never be easy as there will always be players coming up to keep you running scared. I think the 24-second clock will help me. I'm going to love it. That means no stalls, no slowdowns, no control ball. I like to run.

"I expect to report at 205 pounds and like to play at 195. I feel I can jump better, react quicker, feel stronger, and have more strength at that weight."

Does he think he can become an instant starter?

"Every rookie wants to break into the starting lineup," Pete said. "Some are fortunate, and some are less fortunate. I will work my heart out to help the Hawks, and I hope my overall ability, coupled with hard work, dedication, desire, and determination, will help me crack the lineup."

Pete also explained why he dropped out of school during the latter stages of his senior year at LSU.

"First, let me say that in my four years at LSU I have never failed a subject. I have a total of 108 hours of which 98 are credited towards my Business Administration degree. A total of 128 hours is needed for a degree. My grade average was 2.23 of which I am proud because of the circumstances over the past four years. My dad and I deliberated a long time concerning dropping out and not hurting my grade point average, or failing a couple of subjects, making it more difficult to graduate. I hope to get my degree eventually. It's only a matter of applying yourself."

And how was he applying himself to being an instant millionaire.

"I don't know why, as you say, 'having the money now' should make any difference in me, really," Pete said. "I mean, I've never had a lot of it, certainly, but I've never had to want for anything either. Dad's always had a good coaching job (Clemson, North Carolina State, and LSU), and I've always had a place to play basketball. So really, what else did I ever need?

"Oh, I'm sure my dad's had the same dream but he's had it for me. He's not like a lot of fathers you hear about. I mean, his pride isn't so much in me as it is for me. He's proud of what I've achieved because he knows how hard I've worked. It hasn't been easy, and he knows it. Many fathers kinda revel in any glory their sons attain. Some are real pushy, forcing their kid sometimes to play sports just so the father'll feel he's the hero, too. My dad was never like that. From the beginning he's been there to encourage and help me.

"Dad wasn't like that, maybe because he was a pretty doggone good basketball player in his own right. He's still not too bad, either," said Pete with pride in his voice.

"I always hoped Pete would love basketball," said Papa Maravich. "But I was determined to never force it on him. I kinda promised his mother if he liked the sport, good. I'd encourage and help him all I could. If he didn't, though, that'd be okay, too."

But Papa Maravich's dreams were realized as Pete took to the game at an early age and has been addicted ever since.

"I must have been seven or maybe eight when I first really got hooked on the game," says Pete. "We used to have a goal in our backyard wherever we lived—Clemson, Raleigh, anywhere—but I never cared much for basketball then. I remember dad used to go out and shoot by himself all the time. He'd tell us where he was going, but it never dawned on me to go with him. One day I strolled into the backyard, watched for a few minutes, and asked if I could shoot a coupla goals. He said sure and tossed me the ball. Well, I took a shot—and missed! I couldn't understand it," said Pete smiling. "I asked why mine didn't go in, like his had been doing and he said, 'because you're not as good at it as your old man, and you won't ever be!'

"Well, I knew, right then and there, I'd show him. So every day after that I shot, shot, shot—hour after hour after hour. I'd show him. Then, almost before I realized it, I was hooked. Man, I really began to dig it. After that I'd literally open—and close—the local YMCA's. And if I found the doors to the high school or college gyms locked, I'd go through a window. The Harlem Globetrotters have always been a force of inspiration for me. I first saw them as a real small kid and was amazed at how they handled the ball. And their showmanship caught me. It made me wonder why I couldn't have some fun just like they were having. So I began trying to copy some of their stuff. I worked like crazy, and pretty soon I was to where I could do some of their things—like dribble behind my back while running at top speed, and whip passes behind my back and through my legs."

Pete, who has a younger sister Diane, and an older brother Ronnie, a Vietnam veteran, spoke again about his "showtime" routine.

"I love to get a rise out of the crowd. If I can entertain the fans, that's what I want to do, because that's what basketball is all about. But let me get one thing straight, for the umpteenth time—I'm out there to win first. Anything I ever do on the court is for the sole purpose of helping my team. And as far as adapting my college style to the pro game, I don't think I'll have too much trouble. I've always thought passing was the best part of my game, not shooting. Sure, I shot a lot in college, but in the pros there'll be other guys to shoot. I honestly think my passing and ball handling can help the team."

Pete then said he wanted to clear up another matter.

"A lot of people seem to think maybe my childhood wasn't too normal because all I ever did was work toward becoming a good basketball player. Well, I had a wonderful childhood because I was doing what I enjoyed. My mom and dad always permitted me to do what I wanted to do—not just what they wanted. They made sure I had other interests, of course, but they always allowed me enough time to do what I pleased. I wouldn't change one thing if I could go through it again. I'd spend just as much time playing basketball, maybe more. I would only wish, though, we could win a few more games at LSU than we did. I'd want that especially for dad."

Now he was going to get a chance, maybe not for dad, but to win a few games for his new coach—Richie Guerin—and the Atlanta Hawks in his wonderful world of basketball, NBA style.

Pete's Rookie Preseason

Before Pete had even played a preseason game Bob Petit, the ex-LSU all-American and St. Louis Hawks superstar, said that Maravich would bring yet another innovation to the sport. "They'll have to widen turnstiles throughout the sport," the former great said. "He'll be the biggest attraction ever. As far as bringing fans out, he'll do more for the game than anybody ever has.

"The kid'll be a super professional, absolutely," added Petit. "He is truly a tremendous—just great—basketball player."

And then "Hot Rod" Hundley, the wizard of West Virginia University in the mid-50s who was the Maravich of his time, got into the act.

"Whether he'll be able to showboat a little will depend on the situation," said Hundley, who during his college days shot free throws backwards as well as sitting in the stands and cheering himself as his teammates played four on five. "All signs indicate that he'll have trouble. Richie Guerin is hard-headed and believes that every player should fit into a pattern. Pete will have to adjust to Guerin, but as great as Pete is, Guerin will have to do a little adjusting to him."

Hundley, who played pro ball with the Los Angeles Lakers and is now a color commentator on NBA broadcasts, never could adjust to the pro game. "I never did enjoy the pros as much as college," he said. "I couldn't clown around in the pros out of respect to the guys I was playing with and against, although I loosened up my last couple of seasons with the Los

Angeles Lakers."

Hundley then said he felt that "defense would be Pete's biggest problem more than his style of play in the pros. He's going to have to cover somebody, and he's never done that before. And he's not going to shoot 40 times a game or his teammates will kill him."

But it was now nearing "showtime" for Pistol Pete Maravich, the kid who turned down an offer by the Harlem Globetrotters to play with the best of the NBA. In college Pete turned some people on, but in the pros there were already indications that he has turned some of them off.

"Right now I consider him a sub," said Richie Guerin just prior to the preseason. "I think it will be hard for Maravich to break into our starting lineup."

Placed in Guerin's predicament, you have to understand that he would have to contend with a veteran club in addition to the Hawks front office, which would be putting pressure on him to play The Pistol. The dissatisfaction among the Hawks' veterans began when forward Bill Bridges expressed his dissatisfaction with his $50,000 salary in comparison with Maravich's. Bill got little satisfaction from the Hawks' management since he still had a year to go on his contract. And they did not offer to tear it up and sign a more lucrative one.

However some other Hawks made their beefs more discreetly with Walt Bellamy and Jimmy Davis getting raises.

"Nobody's worth the kind of money they are paying anybody," said Guerin. "But it's part of the business. It's part of today. How do you correct it? I don't know, although this kid (Maravich) is going to get a lot of that money back in our exhibition games."

To add further fuel to the Maravich signing fuss, sources in Atlanta reported that Guerin was dead set against the signing. He foresaw trouble brewing, they said. However, the Atlanta coach vehemently denied he was against acquiring Maravich, although he did admit that Pete would have to play the game his way.

"I'm not going to tell him how to pass the ball, behind his back, between his legs, or bounce it off his head," said Guerin. "I've never seen anybody with such control of the ball. But until he's convinced that the simple pass is the best pass, until he's learned what he can do in the pros, Pete will have to feel his way in training camp and exhibitions."

Guerin then added that, "If Pete proves he can play, I'll play him. He's not like any other rookie simply because of all the publicity he has received. But he will be treated in my eyes as I would any other rookie. Every rookie has to prove himself. Even Alcindor was put to the test last year. There was pressure on Alcindor. There'll be pressure on Maravich."

Guerin had previously stated: "There were, perhaps, other players at another position who could have helped us more," at the time Pete was drafted by the Hawks, "but we still got a great player. Plus, we got a player who will be good for the franchise and good for the city. This is, after all a business. And drafting Pete Maravich is good business."

And the business of preseason camp was at hand. Returning were the five previous starters of the year before in which Atlanta had won the Central Division. However, they faltered in the playoffs when scoring leader Hudson went ice cold and playmaker Walt Hazzard broke his wrist.

Now those two were back along with Joe Caldwell, one of the league's top defensive players; Bridges, the team captain and rebounding leader; and Walt Bellamy at center, who had come to the Hawks in mid-year the previous season.

At the Hawks' rookie camp in June the other rookies tried their hardest to rough up Pete, who said he expected it.

"The roughness is good, as it should be," said Pete. "I guess it's sort of like the saga of Wyatt Earp. Everybody wants to beat the fastest gun in the West."

In August at the annual Maurice Stokes Memorial All-Star Game in upstate New York, Maravich made his pro debut, taking 12 shots and making only 4 with Baltimore's Kevin Loughery welcoming Pete by hitting Pete's elbow just slightly on each shot.

"I'd smile, and he'd smile," said Maravich recalling the incident. "I'd say, Okay Kevin; I'll get you back."

But Willis Reed, the New York Knicks star center, did not want any part of Maravich that night, saying to him: "Don't lay any of that stuff of yours on me tonight, Pete, I'm not ready."

Yet Pete was ready, handing out over 10 assists in the game, and when the Hawks' training camp opened in September it was evident The Pistol was on target.

While the other rookies absorbed much rough treatment, Maravich went virtually unscathed by the veterans. One reporter who covered the Hawks said it was no doubt in part because of his economic value to the team, but also "I've got to think it's because they respect him."

Another observer described the veterans reception of Maravich as one of three stages. "In the first stage, when he'd do something spectacular they wouldn't react at all. In the second stage they'd say, 'Woooo, wooo,' but still being Mr. Cool about it. In the third stage, they started patting him on the bottom."

Maravich won over the veterans by hustling, showing no prima donna symptoms, and talking things over with them.

"His quickness is so amazing," said Bridges, "that he avoids those physical contacts," explaining Maravich's elusive way of escaping the pounding of defenders. "His talent is so far ahead of any other rookie I ever saw in camp that it flabbergasts me. I believe he will step into the very first game and play like somebody who's been in the league for five years," said Bridges. "I can only say one thing negative about Pete in practice. I think he's been holding back some of his talents because he doesn't want to be misinterpreted. He doesn't want to look too good yet."

If he was holding back on the court, he was doing likewise off it. "You have to resign yourself to having no private life whatsoever until you retire from the game," said Pete, continuing to be withdrawn off the court. "I have too much time consumed with one thing, basketball, to come out with statements on other subjects."

Maravich's teammates, meanwhile, were noncommittal during training camp about what he was like personally. But on the court, things were not going too well. Caldwell was holding out for a huge increase since Maravich signed (he eventually flew the coup, signing with the Cougars of the rival ABA). And Bridges was suspended and relieved of his captaincy duties briefly in a feud with Guerin.

And then the Hawks lost their first three exhibition games. In the first contest—against Boston—Maravich lost the ball ten times and reverted to some of his college habits, to which

Pete's patented jumper getting set to hit the net against the Philadelphia 76ers, something that was not working during his rookie preseason.

Guerin snapped: "If the kid would quit that free lancing, he could be a helluva basketball player."

　　Pete then hit for 29 points against Philadelphia, connecting on 11 of 22 shots from the floor, but things were going to get worse with Pete himself calling his training camp, "a disaster right from the start."

The Long Season

It all started in training camp. First, Lou Hudson, one of the best shooters in the league, got hurt, then Walt Hazzard, the veteran playmaker, who was expected to help Pete learn the tricks of the pro trade, got off to a terrible start. Joe Caldwell was holding out for more money, and then team captain Bill Bridges drew a suspension for a few hours in an argument with Guerin.

And then there was Pete. "Maybe we could have dug ourselves out of the mess if I had been playing well, but I was terrible," said Pete. "I was trying too hard to be the obedient rookie. For the first time in my life I was thinking on the basketball court instead of just going out there and doing what came naturally."

Then the rumors started to fly concerning dissension on the team with Maravich being the No. 1 choice for causing it. It was sad but also funny in a way. For Maravich had yet to play in a regular season game, and he was already being blamed for wrecking a fine basketball team.

And the situation did not get any better when the exhibition season started. "I was pressing," admitted Pete. "In my very first game as a pro, I committed 10 turnovers while the Boston Celtics as a team made 19."

Pete was getting in plenty of playing time—more than anyone else on the squad, which is what the crowds and newspapermen had come to see. And Pete was also learning his trade, too. "But I was too eager to please," says Pete. "I was rushing my shots, throwing the ball away, and after five preseason games I was barely hitting 40 percent from the field."

After 12 exhibitions the Hawks had a 4-8 record, and then it was time for the regular season.

"I was totally psyched out by the time of our opening game of the season," says Maravich.

Then things turned ever worse in the regular season with Caldwell jumping to the ABA and the Hawks stumbling.

"Probably the biggest trouble we were having was with outsiders," says Pete. "The press particularly. It was the same story everywhere we went. 'See the Bulls play Pete Maravich,' read the ads. Sportswriters were saying all kinds of things about dissension among the Hawks and putting the blame on me for all of it."

A Detroit newspaperman wrote that Maravich was uncooperative with reporters.

"What really happened," said Pete, "was that I didn't have time for an interview then because as a rookie I had to get taped before the veterans. Then another time, after a bad game in Boston, I stayed in the shower too long to suit a writer, and he blistered me the next morning."

But Pete says the best example of his troubles with the press came earlier in the season in New York after dropping a 128-119 decision to the Knicks.

"It had been my first regular season game as a pro at Madison Square Garden, and with Walt Frazier guarding me I'd had a good night: 40 points, 5 assists, some passing that had turned on the crowd. But the big star for us that night was Bill Bridges who held Dave DeBusschere to 12 points and 5 rebounds, scoring 21 points and pulling down 20 rebounds himself."

After the game the writers swarmed to the dressing room and went to Bridges, said Pete. "But guess what the first question was? Right. 'What did you think about Maravich tonight?'

"From that night on I went into hiding," says Pete. "I would stay in the showers for as long as 30 minutes, hoping the writers would just go away. What the hell, I figured, if they're going to draw their own conclusions when we're bad, let 'em draw their own conclusions when we're good."

But Pete still remained in the limelight wherever he went. It seemed everybody wanted to get a glimpse of this wonder who at the age of 20 signed such a lucrative contract and was capable of miracles on the court.

"We'd get off a plane," said Maravich, "and there would be a television crew waiting for me. I'd get in the middle of a crowd and look straight ahead and walk as fast as I could. When we got to the hotel I would go to my room, lock the door, and shut off all calls until time for the game.

"I'd just lie on the floor," said Pete, "staring at the ceiling until three or four in the morning in pure agony, and it was on one of those occasions that I had a heart-to-heart talk with myself. I started thinking about how I had decided when I was still in grade school that I was going to become a star in the NBA; about how I had devoted my life since then to basketball; about the thousands of hours I had spent learning to pass the ball behind my back; about how loose and good I had felt until I joined the Hawks."

That was when Pete decided to change his way of thinking, do his own thing. The other way had not worked, maybe this way would.

There were still 30 games remaining in the season when Pete sat down and had his little talk with himself.

"From then on I felt like I owned the world," says Maravich. "All of a sudden it was like being back at LSU, doing my own thing—giving it the behind-the-back pass, following my instincts, winning and playing to the fans at the same time—and I felt alive again. The team began to play together, and to win. There was a little irony in it, because while I was trying hard to work into the system I was being accused of wrecking the team. But now it was the other way around."

During those final 30 games of his rookie season Maravich averaged nearly 30 points, and the Hawks won 12 of the final 17 games to make the playoffs once again.

Pete does not talk very much about his rookie year, saying simply: "It's over the dam. It happened, I went through it, and now I'm trying to make it a blank in my memory." He admits that it would have been simpler to come into the league with no publicity and a lot less money and sometimes says he wishes he

A pensive Pete during a rare moment on the bench, which is where he spent much of his time when he first joined the Hawks.

had been just another draft pick, but he does not ask or want people to feel sorry for him.

He says it was obvious that there was animosity around the league, when he received only six of 192 votes for the Rookie of the Year balloting by the players. Pete says he even thought about sending telegrams to those six players who voted for him, but he did not know who they were and he really could not care less. "I'm just happy to have the year behind me," he says.

But although it was a frustrating year, Pete admits he learned quite a bit, especially about playing defense and adjusting to new teammates.

"I also learned that there are some moves you can make under the basket in college that you can't make against the bigger and quicker guys in the NBA," says Pete. "But I don't think I learned that much mechanically about playing basketball. I've always had the utmost confidence in my ability. It's the only thing I've ever really wanted to do, and my self confidence was the one thing that saved me from disaster."

It was a disaster of sorts for the Hawks, however, who finished with a 36-46 record and only through the grace of expansion and a favorable division made the playoffs.

But once there, the New York Knicks ripped them four games to one. Once again the problems for the team fell mostly on the shoulders of one Pete Maravich. "You don't know what I've been through," said Pete after the final playoff loss. "I could have done without this year in my life very easily. It's not worth it, but I'm being very well paid."

Pete thought earlier that making the playoffs would solve some of the woes of the season. "If we could get in the playoffs," he said, "it would really mean success for the whole season—it's been such a sad season. I think eventually the team will keep plugging hard enough to get something together. If everybody would get together and forget any type of thing that ever had been bugging them and we could just get on the court and play, I think we would have a great opportunity."

But it did not work out that way. The New York Knicks took care of that. Yet, win or lose in that first season Maravich did bring out the fans.

"Teenage girls go bananas over Pete," said a Hawks spokesman.

"We knew Pete would put people in the place," said owner Tom Cousins. So much so that Cousins and Atlanta mayor Sam Massell announced shortly thereafter that a $17 million coliseum would be built with the Hawks vacating Alexander Memorial Coliseum, the home of Georgia Tech basketball with a seating capacity of only 7,000.

Naturally, the new arena was dubbed "the House that Pete built."

But Pete took it in stride and reflected on his rookie year. "I've progressed, really, about as far as I'm going to," he said. "Anybody who comes into the NBA has a real tough adjustment to make—I sometimes think it's overemphasized. There are so many great ball players you just have to try to mingle in with them. I'm happy the way I've been playing this past month. I don't think I could have done any better in any area. I'm real happy with the way I've progressed."

To Maravich, there were two major adjustments from the college game—the arduous schedule and blending in with the veteran Hawks.

"It's pretty tough for any individual to come in here and try to flow smoothly with a group of guys who have been playing so long, because they seem to know each other's moves on and off the court."

And quite naturally, some of Pete's moves were too tough for his teammates to figure out at first. He often hit unsuspecting Hawks on the shoulder with passes, or sometimes missed them completely.

"I guess the main reason it took me so long," says Pete, "was because I wasn't putting in hardly any time at all at the beginning of the season. And automatically, reporters said 'He hasn't been able to adjust.' But when you're not playing, you're not going to be able to adjust.

"There's been a tremendous amount of pressure on me—and it comes from all areas, the news media, the fans, it even comes from the players, themselves. Because when somebody signs this type of contract you automatically are going to have resentment. I guess that's part of human nature. That's just something you have to adjust to, too.

"There's nothing you can really do about it. You try to earn respect and maybe have them accept you as what you are.

Once this is done then everything seems to work out. But the pressure is really tremendous."

And most of that pressure Maravich created by just being Pete Maravich, the rich rookie from Pennsylvania and the campus of LSU with $1.9 million in his pockets. However, the Hawks management must share some of the blame, along with the press who gave extended coverage every time The Pistol packing rookie made a move.

"We didn't try to extend beyond ourselves and become a team," said Bridges, the team captain, and one of the players who rebelled against Pete at the start. It was almost too late before we finally realized what was happening and moved forward as a team....We lost everything—the battle and the war—but think we'll be better off for it."

Yet not all of what happened to Pete Maravich when he entered the pro ranks was unexpected, since he and his father had been somewhat of a controversial pair during their three years together at LSU.

Pete's First Pro Game

"Watch the Milwaukee Bucks play Pete Maravich in his pro debut." That was all that was heard on ABC-TV commercials for two weeks prior to Pete's first regular season game as a pro. Hardly any mention was made of the fact that the Hawks were playing the defending National Basketball Assocation champions who boasted a fair cast themselves, including Jabbar and Oscar Robertson.

"I didn't get much sleep the night before," Pete recalls.

Then the day was on hand, and there was the $1.9 million heralded rookie, seated at one end of the bench as the Hawk veterans started the game. Pete finally went in at the end of the first quarter with Atlanta ahead by 10 points—a perfect time for the fantastic rookie from LSU to make his debut.

It had been speculated before the game and confirmed by Coach Richie Guerin that Maravich would get to play about 30 minutes. More if he played well, less if he did not. Pete played 22 minutes.

When he entered the contest, there was a small cheer from the crowd, and he looked rather lost at the beginning. Guerin was screaming from the bench, trying to help out. "Over! Over!" he yelled, waving Maravich to one side or the other of the court.

"Come in!" he screamed; then, "Go back! For God's sake, Pete, go back!"

Guerin was almost as good a show off the court as Pete was on it.

Pete was zigging instead of zagging and drifting about, apparently lost, like a kid playing the sport for the first time. Then he started to settle down, and Lou Hudson and Walt Hazzard got hot, so Pete was content to feed them the ball.

Then it happened, the magic of Maravich sprang alive for the first time.

Pete was crouching and weaving near the Bucks foul line on defense while Milwaukee was trying to work the ball into Jabbar. Suddenly the ball went into the middle, Pete's left hand went up, flashed out, and snagged the ball. With all the action going the other way, Maravich sprang loose and was off in the other direction heading for the Hawks basket. He was now a dribbling blur, all alone about 18 feet from the basket and no Hawk to pass to.

He screeched to a halt as one Buck went flying past him, leaped straight up and—swish—two points. The patented, off-balance Pete Maravich jump shot had gone in, and the crowd went wild. He tried 12 other shots during the game and connected on only two more, but he is the type of athlete who excites even when missing.

"When I finally got into the game and ran down the court one time," said Pete, "I wanted to come out immediately. My legs felt like spaghetti, my hands like ping-pong paddles. I couldn't even take the ball and dribble it. I hit on 3 out of 13 shots from the field, we got wiped out, and it was an omen of things to come."

Pete said he felt he would not be a starter right away, and he was right. He sat on the bench and played in spots for the first three weeks, learning all the time. It was an odd feeling for The Pistol, whose only experience at sitting on the bench in the past had been on the rare occasions when he fouled out of a game in college.

"It was a strange feeling, being on the sidelines for the first time in your life, and I hardly knew what to do with myself," said Pete. "I was getting in for about 20 minutes a game, but even then I was contributing very little to the team. It went like that for a dozen games."

During that span Pete averaged 13.6 points. He then missed Game No. 14 with a slight injury and was told by Guerin that he would be a starter in the next game.

"It's funny," explained Pete. "But that's when my real problems began. I don't really know how to explain it. I wasn't doing that badly on the court."

In spite of the intense pressure on him Maravich scored 23, 28, 32, 32, 32, and 40 points in his first six games, and he says his ball handling and defense was getting better. During the next 10 games, however, with the season nearing the halfway point, things started to disintegrate for the Hawks and Pete.

Joe Caldwell jumped to the Carolina Cougars of the rival American Basketball Association, Pete had become a starter and drawing the attention of the fans and the press, and the Hawks were stumbling along with a 9-21 record. Not exactly what was expected of the team that had captured the Central Division Conference the season before.

"My morale and everybody else's on the team had hit bottom," says Maravich.

Superstar In The Making

In his three years at LSU, which before the arrival of Maravich had been known for football and little else, Pete had been accused of being all the things a basketball star should not be—hothead, hot dog, ball hog, and gunner. And Press did little to shackle the talents of his son. In fact he could be heard from the bench shouting during games to Pete: "Shoot the ball, Pete. Don't pass it. Shoot."

And once Press snapped at a reporter who was trying to compare Maravich with Bob Cousy: "Cousy never saw the day he had moves like Pete."

At any rate he did help make a youngster into a player who excited the whole nation by the time he was a senior at LSU. And when his fabulous college career was over, Pete managed to shoot more and score more than anyone in college history, averaging 38.1 shots a game and 44.5 points a contest. But he was truly exciting, probably more so when he had the ball in his magical hands, than when shooting, admitting that if he had a choice of setting up a basket with a simple pass or a mind-boggling one he would prefer the latter.

"All that common stuff—dribbling down straight, chest pass, bounce pass, fundamental stuff like that—that's going out of basketball," he said.

But one has to admit that the Maraviches brought LSU basketball from oblivion to a National Invitation Tournament berth in his senior year after compiling an 18-10 record. And his teammates agreed that if LSU was to win, Pete had to shoot.

And shoot he did. He had a 26 for 57 night. A 17 for 48 night and a spectacular 22 for 30 night. Once on a trip out West, Oregon State felt they had a way to stop The Pistol. Foul him. This did not disturb Pete as he calmly dropped in 30 of 31 free throws in the game.

He led the nation in scoring for three years, was an all-American all three seasons, and in his senior year was named College Player of the Year.

Off the court, coeds followed him around constantly. Like many a wild youth he got into some minor scrapes with the law with reckless driving charges. But his private life has been guarded like the vaults of Fort Knox, and this complex young man only opens up on a basketball court.

"When he's on the floor," said Lou Carnesseca, of St. John's, New York, during the NIT, "you forget everything else to watch him. He's like an artist. Always creating."

Carnesseca may have had in mind the game Pete had against the University of Georgia during his junior year. It was the final game of the season at the Athens, Georgia, gymnasium, and Pete had led LSU back from 15 points behind to a tie after regulation time, then another tie after the first overtime.

Pete then took charge in the second five-minute period, and with 90 seconds left he decided "to put on a dribbling exhibition." He dribbled behind his back, between his own legs, and defenders as well. The Georgia home crowd even forgot itself and began to cheer the floppy haired Maravich.

Then with three seconds left, Maravich showed his amazing flair for the unbelievable. He dribbled toward his own bench, and with his back to the basket, tossed in a 35-foot hook shot—hardly disturbing the net, as the buzzer sounded. The basket gave Pete 58 points for the night, and as Pete said: "The 14,000 people just sat there stunned."

But his final college act during LSU's three games in the NIT in New York's Madison Square Garden were somewhat different. First off, Pete was hobbled by injuries, there were defenders everywhere Pete looked, and in the semifinal round an excellent Marquette team blew LSU off the court.

In the months that followed, Maravich dropped out of school, passed up a banquet in which he was presented a second straight trophy as LSU's premier athlete, and turned down the

Harlem Globetrotters offer to become the first white on the all-black team, famed for all the things Maravich does best.

One person associated with the Globetrotters was overheard to say about Pete, "If he weren't white, I'd swear he was one of us."

Pete's College Years

It was a winter night in 1971, a Monday night in March to be exact, and Pistol Pete's fabulous college career was over, much too quickly for LSU rooters, but it was finally over. In his honor Maravich was saluted along with his teammates at the annual Tipoff Club banquet in Baton Rouge. Showered was more appropriate for what happened that night.

Pete was presented with awards, citations, accolades, and words of praise of the era that had just ended, closing out his career on a triumphant note. The mayor of Baton Rouge proclaimed it "Pete Maravich Day," and more than 700 persons jammed into LSU's Union Hall, to stand in awe of this living legend who brought basketball to a part of the country where only football had survived before. He received the Leadership Award, the Most Valuable Player award, the award for most assists over the season, and along with roommate and fellow guard Jeff Tribbett, named permanent co-captains.

For Pete it was a last hurrah for the three-time all-American who helped rescue LSU from the doldrums of a 3-23 campaign the season before he made his varsity debut, to a 22-10 record and a berth in the National Invitation Tournament after his senior year.

"It's really unbelievable," said Maravich of the two-hour banquet. "I remember when I was a freshman and I came to a banquet here, and there were something like 77 people. This is unbelievable."

He was given three standing ovations, then was mobbed for

over an hour afterwards, signing autographs. And he signed every last one, too.

Demonstrations like the one at the banquet were nothing new to Maravich, though. In fact it was nothing compared to the night of January 31 when 11,856 fans almost tore up LSU's Agricultural Center when he became the highest scorer in college basketball history.

"Oh heavens! Honest to goodness," said LSU coach Press Maravich. "When he hit that 40th point...boom! They (the fans) almost tore this place up, man. You wouldn't believe it. We're lucky we all didn't get crushed! The minute Pete's (23-foot) jumper fell through (4:43 left to play), complete bedlam broke loose! Honest to goodness, I've never seen anything like it in my life," said Press. "We had 40 security guards there. And they couldn't even control the people," he added, still amazed and proud of that moment.

What that basket did was wipe away forever the name of Oscar Robertson, who from that moment on became the former collegiate all-time scoring king, replaced by a skinny youngster with the funny last name. Pete blazed his name into the record books during LSU's 109-86 triumph over Mississippi and at the final buzzer had popped in 53 points, giving him 2,987 career points, snapping Robertson's record of 2,973.

Maravich had opened his senior year 687 points behind the "Big O" and in 14th place among all-time scorers. He was to finish his career with 3,667 points.

"My ears are still ringing," said Press. "When he got up to 39, those people started screaming: 'One, one, one...' It almost drove me batty."

The 6-foot-5, 185-pounder was "very tense" for the next couple of minutes according to his father. "He was kinda forcing his shots—missing four jumpers in a row. Down court the fifth time, though, he seemed a little more relaxed. Then...bingo! He got it!

"You'd have thought somebody had dropped the atomic bomb, or something, all those people streaming out of the stands like that. And that noise...oh, that noise," he says. "I've still got a headache.

"I'll tell you, though. It was the happiest moment of my life. Pete said it was his happiest, too. I'd have never—not in a

Pete scoring the basket that made him college's all-time leading scorer, snapping Oscar Robertson's mark of 2,973 points.

million years—dreamed when he was young that someday he'd accomplish that. But it's an everlasting credit to a great basketball player...a great basketball player."

Only a few days later Alabama coach C. M. Newton, LSU's next opponent, was talking about Maravich, in awe.

"He's got almost anybody he plays broke and in the hole before you even play him," said Newton. "We're as good as down 47-0, really, right now...two days before they even get here. You know Pete's gonna get that many—or more—points. And besides, we have to put three or maybe even four of our boys' totals together to get 47 points," said Newton. "In my mind there's no room for doubt that Pete'll be a great pro. He's the best offensive basketball player I've ever seen for a couple of reasons," Newton added.

"It's not so much, really, that Pete's just a great shooter, either. There have been many great shooters. He's in a class by himself, though, in that he has the ability to create his own scoring opportunities. This facet of his game, I feel, has long been overlooked. Pete doesn't depend on other people's picks. He doesn't have to. The speed with which he comes down court and his moves do that for him. He'll fake the defense in such a manner it will be his 'pick.' Watch him sometime," said Newton.

Then Newton spoke of his passing ability, which he noted was possibly even more fantastic than his shooting.

"He passes off a lot more than most people would believe. He draws the people to him, naturally, and is apt to as not flip off to somebody else. He's a team man, first and foremost, regardless of what anybody would lead you to believe. He's averaging what—48-point something. Okay, LSU's team average is in the high 90s. That should tell you something about its balance," said Newton.

"But stopping LSU? Well, that's possible," he said. "But stopping Pete...Well, now, that's something else again."

And it was possible. Alabama's Crimson Tide came up with an upset and hung one on LSU 106-104, but like he said, stopping Pete was another story. What Pete did was score 69 points—the most he had ever scored in a college game, which still stands as a Southeastern Conference record. The Pistol took 57 shots and connected on 26 from the field, a .456 percentage, and hit on 17 of 21 free throws, sending the Alabama crowd of 15,043 home in amazement at this fantastic youngster's ability.

A couple of weeks earlier Pete, with his long brown hair flopping in his face but minus sideburns, was talking about scoring records and the lack of hair coming down the side of his face.

"I can't grow any," he said smiling. "I don't even have to shave much. Just here on my chin and above my lip, but you could rub it off with a towel," he said laughing.

But his scoring records will take a bit more longer to rub off, if, in fact, anyone ever comes along to accomplish that remarkable feat.

About his shooting and scoring ability, Pete is not bashful, saying: "I know I can get open, that's no problem. I've just got to hit the shot. But I don't think about the offensive pressures on me. I don't go out there thinking I have to score 45."

It was after a 79-70 loss to Auburn in which Pete had tossed in 44 points, and as he changed from his purple and gold LSU uniform into a striped shirt, maroon slacks, black socks, and tassled loafers, Pete reflected.

"One of these nights," he said. "Everything is going to go in. If I take 40 to 45 shots, I'm going to hit 40. I just know it's coming.

In the Auburn game it was not one of those nights. Pete had 46 field goal attempts and made but 18. His father termed it a "bad performance."

Pete was more outspoken. "I just stunk, that's what it amounted to. I had the shots, I was just short."

Pete never did achieve that night when "everything was going in," but he certainly came close against Clemson, earlier in that season. Pete hit on 22 of 30 shots for a 73 percent shooting night as LSU ran to a 111-103 victory. Maravich added 5 of 8 free throws for a 49-point evening, while also picking up nine assists in addition to giving the home folks in Clemson, South Carolina, something to discuss at the next morning's breakfast.

But shooting is one of the things Pete does best and does not mind talking about, especially since most of his shots fall into the 25-foot or longer category.

"Out there, from 25, 30 feet, that's no strain," he says.

"My percentage out there is just as good as it is from 15 feet. Most of my shots against Auburn were from the right side, but that doesn't mean anything.

"One time a scout from Tulane went back to tell their coach that I only went to my right. I forget who we were playing in that game, but they were giving me the right. When we played Tulane, they shaded me to the right, so I went to my left and got 54."

But says Pete, "I'd still rather win. You can have all the points, I'd rather win and play in New York in the NIT."

And the points came in buckets for Pete, who averaged 44.2 points a game as a junior, 43.8 as a sophomore. But LSU only had 14-12 and 13-13 records.

His senior year had been different though, although he increased his scoring average to 46.6. LSU finally had a winning season, and a hoped-for NIT bid.

"It's always been a dream of mine to play in New York," said Pete. "New York has the kind of basketball fans I like to play for. The spectators there eat it, pray it, live it. The fans there look like they all played it. Look how the Knicks get 19,500 every game. Talk about team basketball, those guys are something else."

After the NIT, all the talk was about the pros, where would Maravich play, the NBA or ABA. Pete did not know then, saying only, "All I know about the pros is that I've got to put on a few pounds."

But no matter which team got the services of the acrobatic Maravich, one thing was for certain. He would arrive with two pairs of gray sweat socks which flopped as much as his hair.

"They're not dirty," said Pete of his famed socks, which have found a home in the Helms Basketball Hall of Fame. "They're gray, that's their color. I put 'em in a washer. But they're torn, they've got holes in them. I've had 'em for four years. They're not a trademark, and I'm not superstitious. They just felt so comfortable when I put 'em on four years ago that I've kept them."

Pete also likes to talk basketball after each game, yearning to learn even more about the game he loves so much.

"I like to go home and talk basketball with my father until 4 or 5 in the morning," he said after the Auburn loss. "But I don't want to go home tonight. I think I'll get something to eat and hit the sack in the dorm. I'm a pretty poor loser."

But Pete has always been a poor loser, striving for perfection each time he hits the court and is never satisfied with his performance.

During his junior year at LSU, a Southern official who worked many of LSU's games had this observation of The Pistol.

"The boy's got to learn to settle down. He's a great talent. But sometimes he tends to be a crybaby. He thinks you can't block a shot or knock the ball out of his hands without committing a foul. He better mature before he gets to the pros."

He also criticized Pete's father and coach, Press, saying the LSU mentor should put a halter on his star rather than sympathize with him.

"Sure, anyone's going to miss a call now and then," the official said. "But the calls even up. You get out of Baton Rouge, and all you hear is how you're protecting Pete."

And some of the statements may have been true, since the Maraviches, Pete and Press, were hit with eight technical fouls in LSU's first 13 games that season before the pair calmed down for the remainder of the year. But the official pointed out that Pete's game was starting to settle down and maybe his temper too.

Yet in all fairness to Pete, every opponent he faced was double and triple teaming him, pounding him and getting away with murder literally, especially when LSU took to the road. Again, that is the price of fame, and Pete was paying for it.

"Pete is not forcing the shots he did as a sophomore," said the official, who had watched Maravich throughout his career. "His passing is as great as it has ever been. He simply has to curb his temper—and his father should lend a hand."

Some observers feel that Pete's personality, sometimes flippant, along with his temper—may have cost him a shot at making the U.S. Olympic squad after his sophomore season. First off, Pete and John Bach, the Penn State coach, who headed the Olympic trials, did not hit it off.

"I wasn't too happy about Pete trying out," said Press. "I knew there would be some politics involved. But Pete felt it was a once-in-a-lifetime chance, and he didn't want to miss out on it."

Pete's failure to make the team shook him up for a little while, but it did not injure his pride. He used the time when the Olympic Games were played to go on a weight program and add 10 pounds to his skinny frame, going to 192 pounds for his junior year.

Press admits that patience is not one of Pete's virtues.

"He never wants to take the long way home," says Press. "He doesn't like to hit the open man unless the man is under the goal. And he can't seem to shake off a defeat."

As a freshman Pete's and LSU's unbeaten season was ruined by a 75-74 loss to the Tennessee frosh. In that contest, trailing by two with eight seconds left, Pete drew a one-and-one foul and stepped to the free throw line confidently. He made the first but missed the second, and LSU had absorbed its only loss of the year.

Press became concerned when he could not find Pete after the game—and only later learned that he had left the gymnasium and walked two miles to the hotel in Knoxville, Tennessee.

But the sport has always had a hold on Pete. Once he played with a heavily-taped ankle that required him to wear a size 16 shoe instead of his normal 12½. He responded with a 42-point effort. Another time he played with a temperature of 104 and scored 47 points.

As a freshman against Mississippi Southern, in the first half he sustained a cut above his eye that needed nine stitches. He came back and finished with 42 points.

And so it is onto New Orleans now for the youngster who holds 12 NCAA scoring records, scored 50 points in his college freshman debut, and closed out his regular season college career with 41 points against Georgia.

It is a long way for this NBA player's son who was dribbling a basketball when he was three years old, spinning a ball on his finger at 8, and at 12 declared he was going to make a living playing pro basketball.

And scoring championships do not seem to matter that much either for Maravich.

"I've led all kinds of leagues," says Pete. "Personal things like leading the league don't get you a cup of coffee. My obsession is to be on a championship team. As soon as I am, I'll retire. Definitely. Right then. Because then I will have been successful. I'm really only happy when I'm winning. Losses always bother me."

And so the championship journey begins for Pistol Pete Maravich and the New Orleans Jazz.

Poppa Press And Scotty Robertson

The father and son act the Maraviches performed at LSU ended in 1970, and after a year without Pete at the Baton Rouge school Papa Maravich went his merry way back to the mountains of North Carolina as the coach at tiny Appalachian State.

In his heart he probably will always search for another Pistol Pete but really does not expect to find another one. In fact he did not find the first one. He grew him, groomed him, and guided him, and what Pete became is what Press wanted him to become. Good or bad, Press Maravich got what he asked for, and he has no regrets.

"I miss Pete," says Press. "He's a great son."

But the criticism was there while the two displayed their act at LSU. One veteran coach was outwardly critical, saying, "I think it was a disgrace what he did with that kid. No player should take 40 or 50 shots a game, especially the coach's son. How can that be good for the kid? How can it be good for the rest of the team?

Yet Press still maintains the same view he did then, claiming if he had a superstar he would repeat his actions.

"I'd do the same thing, and nobody would say anything about the coach if the boy isn't his son. I believe in utilizing the talent that's available. If I have a great basketball player, I use him to the fullest, and Pete was a great basketball player. If you give him the ball, something is going to happen. The things he did with a basketball I would like to see again."

The elder Maravich says, for instance, football coaches spend years looking for a quarterback who can throw the ball, and when they find one they let him throw 40 or 50 times a game and nobody says anything.

Then there was this clinic a few years back in a little town called Bowie's Creek, North Carolina, and Pete was there, says Maravich. There were 2,000 people at the clinic and maybe there have never been 2,000 people in Bowie's Creek again, but they came there to see Pete. That is the end, to Press Maravich, that justifies the means.

But it has been tough on Papa Press these last few years without Pete around.

"I've been together with the kid since I broke him in at the age of seven," he says. "We've been very close, always discussing things. Basketball, school, everything. When he was little, just sopping up basketball at home or wherever I was coaching, I used to give him all sorts of drills—spinning the ball on his finger, bopping it with his head, fun things."

But Press says that is past now, and he would not change a thing if he had to do it over.

"I'd go the same way. He's so great I enjoyed coaching him. We had no trouble relating to each other or relating to the team. He'll never get big-headed. That's because he understands he's not bigger than the game. I taught him, and I teach the rest of the kids that the one thing they must recognize is each other's ability, to understand their relationship to each other."

And for Press it was easy to relate. He played four years in the leagues that preceded the National Basketball Association and one year for Pittsburgh in 1946-47, the year the NBA was formed. He later coached at Clemson, North Carolina State, LSU, and now at Appalachian State.

The older Maravich was introduced to basketball in Sunday School in his hometown of Aliquippa, Pennsylvania, where he spent the hours between midnight and 8 a.m. working in the steel mills before going to high school.

"I attended three Bible classes every Sunday," he recalls, "just to get a chance to play."

He made the best of his chances and ultimately received a scholarship to Davis and Elkins in West Virginia and once scored 29 points against then mighty Long Island University. World

"The Pistol" whizzing past Detroit's Bob Lanier for a two-pointer.

War II interrupted his schooling, but he returned to school later on the GI bill and later earned another degree at West Virginia Wesleyan, taught English, played pro ball, and worked the steel mills once more before Davis and Elkins offered him his first coaching position.

But he refuses to take any of the credit for Pete's rise to stardom.

"He got where he is by hard work, not heredity," says Papa. "He has great instinctive ability. He's graceful and quick and has tremendous reactions. Sure you can say I'm just a proud father talking, but ask people who have played against him. I have no idea what he'll do with the ball when he gets it, but whatever he does it will bring you out of your seat."

And Pete will get a chance to get his newest coach, Scotty Robertson, out of his seat. The New Orleans coach has never seen Pete play much in person, and until Maravich signed with the Jazz, Robertson had never even spoken to his All-Star guard.

"I saw Pete play in college a few times and some in the pros, twice during the 1973-74 season," says Robertson, a 44-year-old newcomer to the pro coaching ranks after 23 years of high school and college coaching.

"I had never met Pete until I talked with him just after I was appointed coach, and that was on the telephone," says Robertson, who left the head coaching reins at Louisiana Tech, after 10 years at the position.

"But I am a Pete Maravich fan," adds Robertson unequivocally. "I think he can do as many things with a basketball as anybody in the game today. I think he's definitely one of the greatest offensive players in the game.

"I'm a fast break offensive coach, and I can't think of anybody in the country I'd rather have handling the basketball for me than Pete. If you could just think up a composite drawing of the perfect player to quarterback our team, you couldn't have found anybody better.

"I've talked with people who know Pete, and they say he is very intelligent and a hard worker," says Robertson, who has a fine track record as an outstanding leader throughout his career. "You know Pete had to work hard to perfect the skills he has," Robertson adds. "And I think Pete is the type of person we're looking for. I saw him just a few times in college, on television the past few years, and two games in person this past year. And this may sound probably a little screwy, but I think Pete has improved his shooting."

Now the obvious question is, how can you improve the shooting of a guy who led the nation for three years in scoring and finished as the second leading scorer in the NBA. But Robertson has the answers.

"There are two different points on the subject," explains Robertson. "1, you're a scorer, and 2, you're a shooter. In college Pete was more of a scorer; now he's a scorer but a better shooter. The difference is he's not getting as many layups now, and his percentage is better as a pro. In college if you're anything as a player and you throw up a lot of shots, you're going to score a lot of points. But Pete is now shooting less and enjoying it more, I think."

Robertson pointed out that "Pete can still score...What I am saying is that I saw films on him recently, and he's got all the offensive moves that make a person a scorer. But his biggest improvement has been that he's shooting better percentage shots and from outside.

"One thing I do know is that Pete Maravich is a super basketball player. He was very fortunate in having a father who had a great knowledge of the game. He's paid the price to be great, and it has enabled him to be where he is today," says Robertson.

"I'm just thrilled to death to have him with our club. He's well liked by the majority of people in our state, and as you know, Pete was instrumental in upgrading basketball here. During Pete's tenure at LSU he and his father got basketball up to where it is today in Louisiana."

The subject reverted back once again to scoring, the thing that made the nation take notice when Maravich was performing his magical act at LSU.

"As for scoring," said Robertson, "what does it mean for Pete to get 37 points a game, he's done that a thousand times. I

Chet Walker of the Chicago Bulls tries futilely to block Pete's jumper from the foul line on a fast break with Norm Van Lier in pursuit.

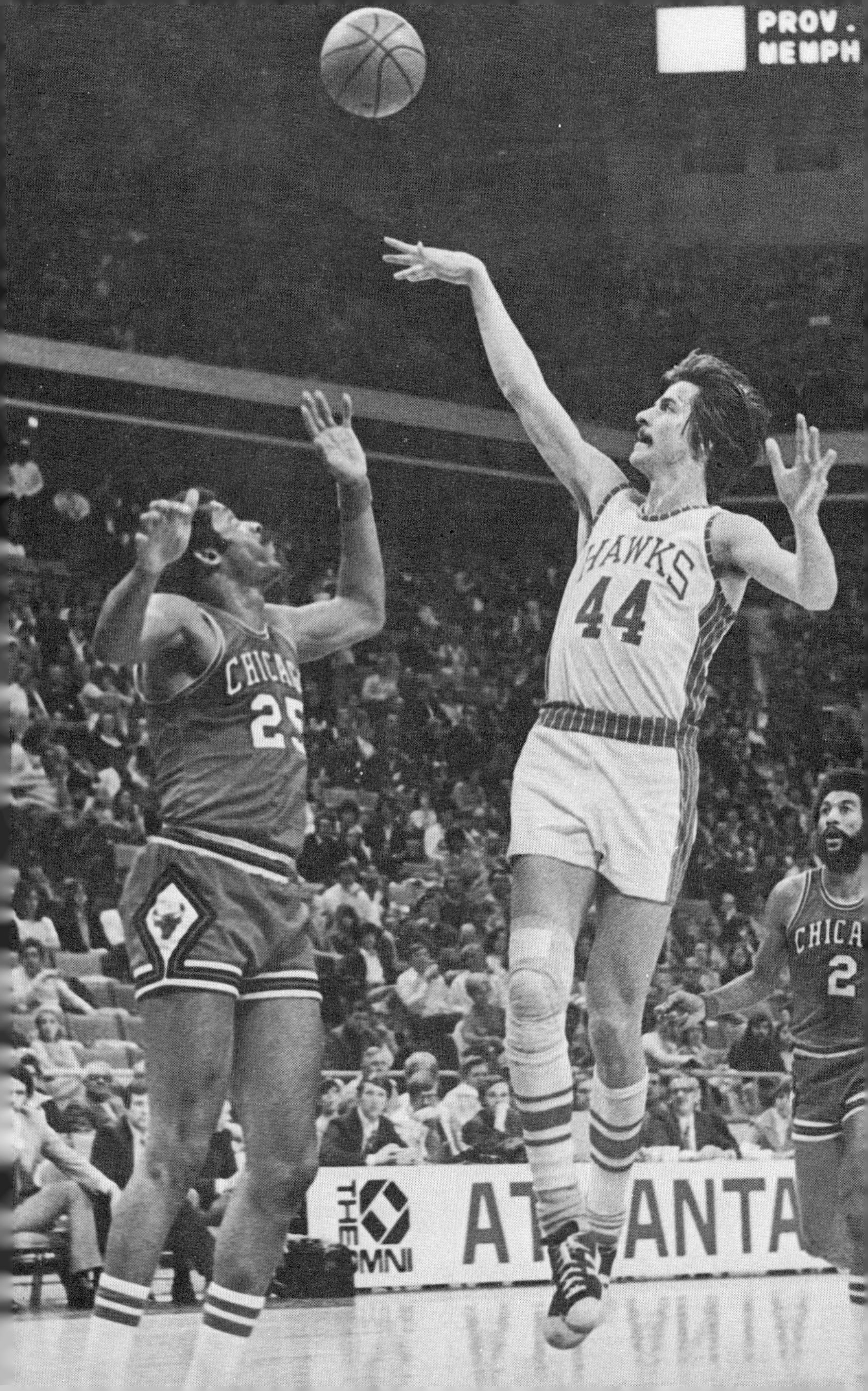
PROV.
MEMPH
HAWKS
44
CHICA
25
CHICA
2
THE OMNI
ATLANTA

believe that he wants the same thing I want and that is to win. Whether he scores 37 or 3 points, it'll be super if we win.

"I want Pete Maravich to shoot the basketball for me everytime he has a good percentage shot. But what you may be forgetting is that Pete Maravich is also an unbelievable ball handler, and he is an unbelievable passer and penetrator.

"All of those things go into the success of a basketball team, and I plan to use his talent for the success of the entire New Orleans organization. We're going to make mistakes. Pete will, I will, but anything that's worth while doesn't come easy. Diamonds are expensive, and you know why, because there's not too many of them."

Robertson then spoke of his coaching theories and how Pete will fit in.

"I think the NBA is a darned tough league from bottom to top. I'm a fast-break coach, but defense is what you win with in the NBA. Pete, in my opinion, played in college for his father. He had all the attention and all the pressure on himself to do the scoring. When that's the case, emphasis is not placed on your defense. It has to be on your mind, 'I can't foul out, I've got to score 30-35 points for us to win.' So defense is not the primary importance to you.

"Here, however, Pete will be called on to be a showman, an offensive player, an assist man and our quarterback. That's what I'm going to call on him to do. Of course, he's going to have to play defense too. But his primary asset is not defense. I plan to take our best assets and use them to our advantage. I don't think Pete's best asset is defense," but Robertson emphasized that, "Pete can play defense."

Robertson says he is excited over "having Pete Maravich as a basketball player," which reminded him of a headline in an Atlanta paper once. "It said 'Hawks fans pay steak prices for hamburger performance,'" recalled Robertson.

"Now I think we owe something to that fan who pays $7. I'm not being critical of the way Pete was coached in Atlanta, but a person pays that money, he deserves to be entertained. And Pete Maravich, to me, is an exciting player. Then the thing everyone asks is, 'Yea, sure, Pete's exciting, but can you win with him?'

"Well my answer is that Pete Maravich is a player of multi

talents, and I say, yes, we can win with him. He has accomplished everything there is to accomplish in the game of basketball. The only thing he wants and I want—is to come up with a winner."

And so Robertson and Pete, it seems, have one common goal, as Maravich often says, "It's all about one thing," pointing to the finger where championship rings are worn.

Maybe someday soon, with Maravich as the cornerstone and Robertson the architect, that dream will become a reality.

Only time can tell.

How To Do It Pete's Way

By Pete Maravich

SHOOTING

The layup: If you're shooting from the right side of the court, jump off with your left foot and push your right knee as high as you can toward the basket. Use your right hand to push the ball softly against the backboard. For left-handers, it is the exact opposite.

Jump shot: Hold the ball with your fingertips, not in the palms of your hand. Try to maintain backspin and follow through with your body and extend your hands and arms after releasing the ball.

PASSING

There are four basic passes: the chest pass, the baseball pass, the overhead pass, and the chest bounce-pass. The main thing in passing is using your fingertips and not the palm of your hand, just like in shooting. Control of the ball is all in the fingertips. The most important thing to remember is never hold the ball in the palms of your hands, never. The only exception is when you are catching a pass, and then only for a fraction of a second should it remain in your palms. For the basic two-handed passes, the ball is held by your fingertips with the fingers evenly spread around the sides and slightly behind the center of the ball.

In passing the ball you have to have backspin on it. This makes the ball go faster, and it is easier to handle for the man catching the ball. To get backspin you have to flick your wrists

Pete looking to pass, holding the ball firmly with two hands.

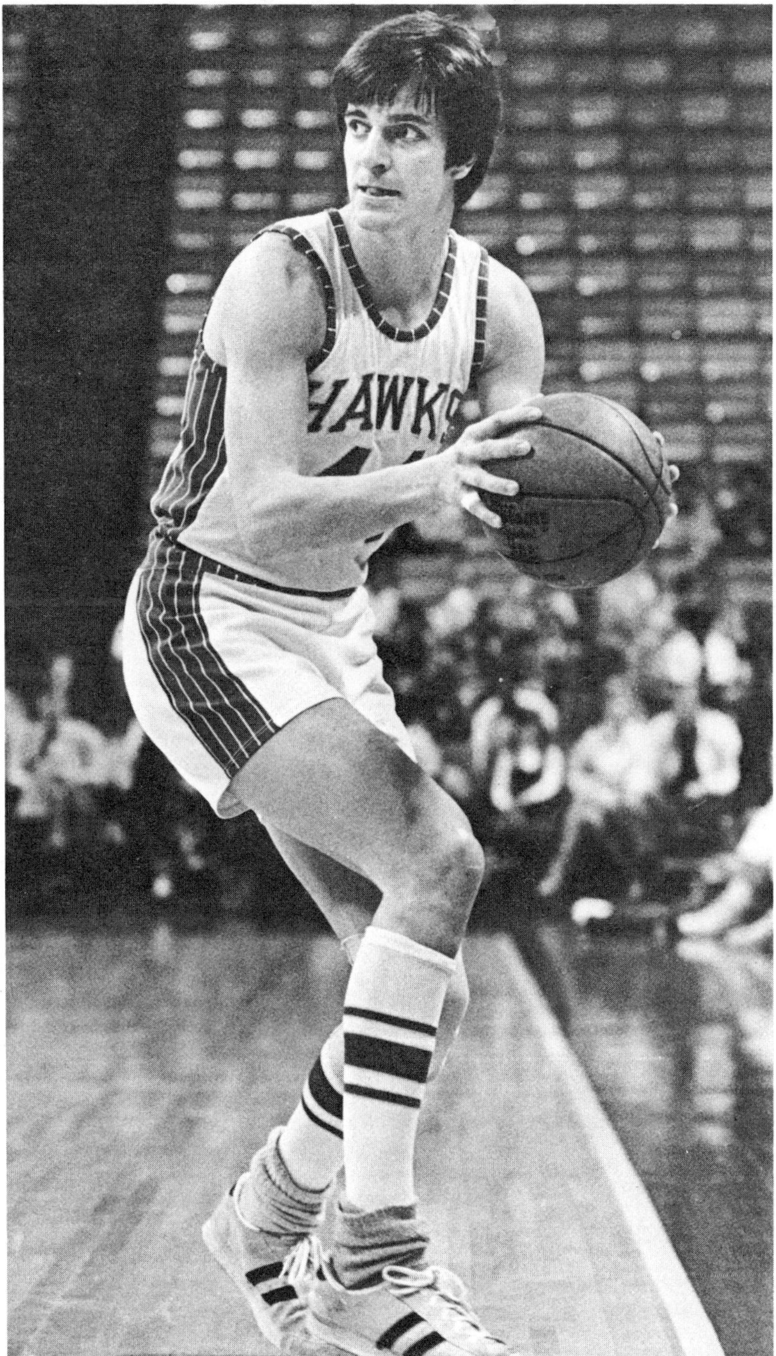
HAWKS

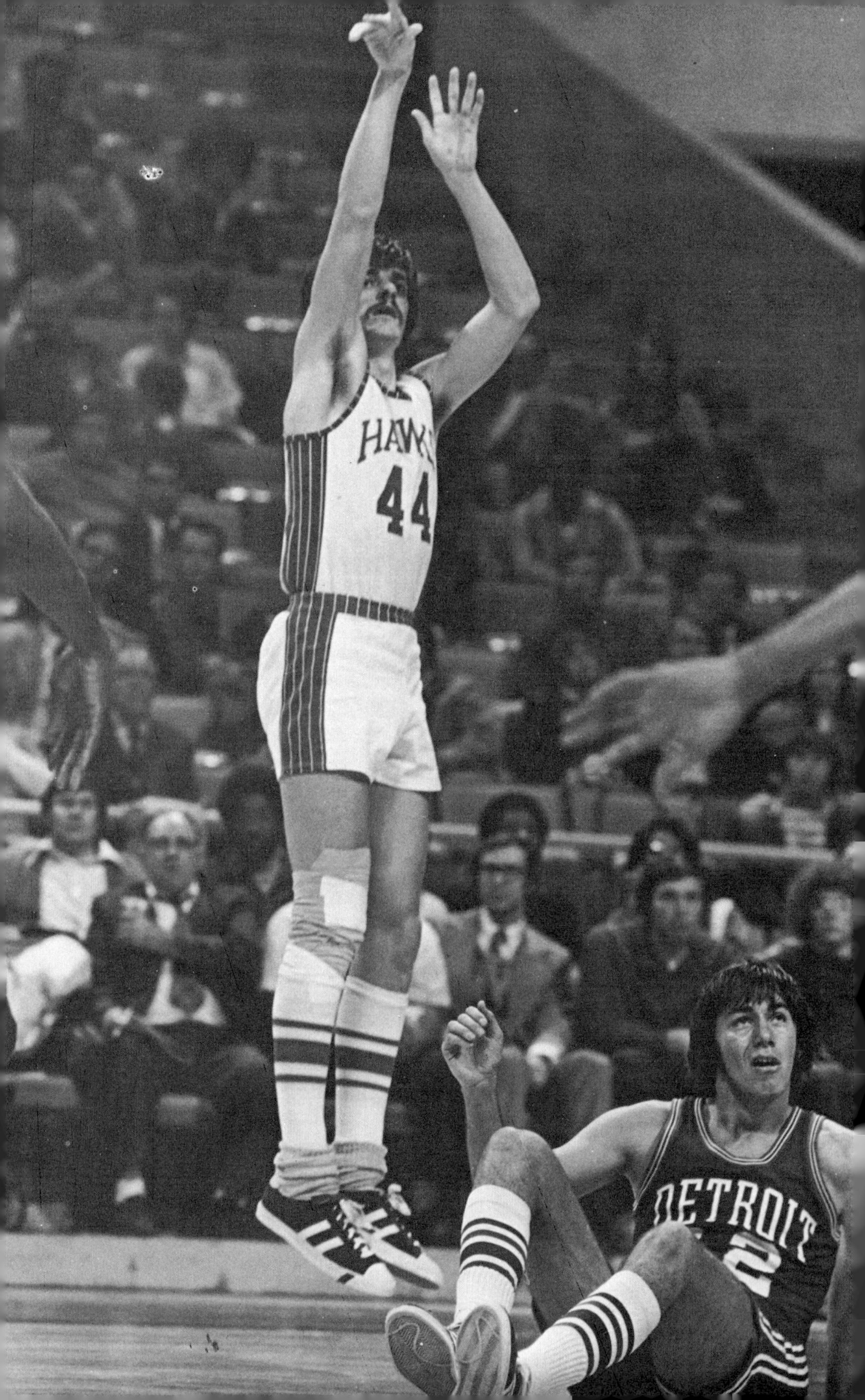
HAWKS
44
DETROIT

when you release the pass. When you throw the ball, just snap your wrists. It's as easy as that.

The follow-through is just as important, extending your hands and arms in the direction you are throwing the pass. Another important thing is never to stand still when passing. Your feet should always be on the move.

The chest pass is used for short passes in which quickness and accuracy are of the utmost importance. The follow-through plays a main role at all times. The proper follow-through is accomplished by bending your knees slightly and bringing your body forward a bit, then taking a short step forward in the direction of the pass. The chest bounce-pass is similar, except you bounce the ball with the intention of hitting your target in the waist.

The overhead pass is similar, doing all the same moves as the chest pass, except the ball is placed over your head. Throwing it with backspin or without it, doesn't make much difference. Whatever is easier for you to do, is the proper way.

The baseball pass is just what it says. You draw the ball back like a baseball pitcher and throw it with one hand. It is usually only used on a long pass when you see a man loose at the other end of the court.

Remember to bring the ball back with your right hand and move your left foot forward to keep your balance, then throw the ball in an overhand motion. Try not to bend your elbow so the ball doesn't curve.

Those are the four fundamental passes which you should master before going into anything fancy such as the behind-the-back pass. I learned how to throw the behind-the-back pass when I was about ten years old. I practiced it by throwing it past a defensive man, facing him all the time. I'd try the pass four or five times a day, then practicing it as I took one step back. I still practice it. That's the only way you will learn any of the passes—by practice and more practice. The same goes for shooting and dribbling.

Pete has just faked Detroit's Jim Mengelt out of his sneakers before popping in a jumper, showing the correct follow through.

Pete showing the correct way to dribble with the ball out in front of him and using only his fingertips.

DRIBBLING DRILLS

I have five basic dribbling drills and I call them Punching the Bag, The Ricochet, The Walking Pretzel, The See-Saw Drill, and the TV Dribble.

In Punching the Bag, your fingertips and feet are the two most important things, as they are in passing, shooting, or handling the basketball. This drill can be done from a squatting or bending position. First you start dribbling the ball about four inches off the floor as fast as you can and just listen to it and continue beating it until it stops on the ground.

The Ricochet is important for developing coordination. You stand up straight with your feet spread about 30 inches apart. Then you throw the ball at a 45-degree angle so that it bounces between your legs and you try to catch it behind your back. You probably won't be able to do this at the beginning, but keep practicing it and soon your back and hands will be in unison. What you have to do when the ball leaves your hands is shift your lower back and hips a bit forward, and move your hands behind your back and into position to catch the ball when it comes back up.

The Walking Pretzel is designed to change hands and feet while you are dribbling. You start by dribbling with your left hand as near to your right foot as possible. Then gradually dribble the ball around your right foot and change hands by dribbling with your right hand. Then without stopping dribble the ball around your left foot, again switching hands. Always in dribbling try to keep the ball as close to the floor as possible. After you've done this drill standing still and have become adept at it, then go on to the same drill but this time while walking.

The See-Saw Drill is a variation of the Walking Pretzel with the only variation coming by bouncing the ball behind your back rather than around your feet. Place the ball behind you and bounce it with both hands, with your hands going up and down in a see-saw manner. First do it standing, and then try it while moving.

Last is the TV Dribble, which I started doing when I was very young and did while watching television in the living room. In this drill you sit on the floor and dribble the ball entirely around your whole body, first in one direction and then in the opposite direction.

When you have mastered these five drills, you ought to be able to control a basketball as well as a professional.

Statistics

NCAA RECORDS HELD BY PETE MARAVICH

SINGLE GAME
Free throws scored:
 30 (31 att.) vs. Oregon State (12-22-69)

SINGLE SEASON
Field goals attempted:
 1,168 (522 made) in 1969-70
Field goals made:
 522 in 1969-70
Points scored:
 1,381 (522 fg, 337 ft) in 1969-70

CAREER
Field goals attemped:
 3,166 (1,387 made) in 1967-70
Field goals made:
 1,387 (3,166 att.) in 1967-70
Points scored:
 3,667 (1,387 fg, 893 ft) in 1967-70

MISCELLANEOUS
Top two-year totals:
 2,509 (951 fg, 607 ft) in 1968-69 and 1969-70
Most points scored as a sophomore:
 1,138 (432 fg, 274 ft) in 1967-68
Most points scored as a junior:
 1,148 (433 fg, 282 ft) in 1968-69

Most points scored at the end of the junior season:
   2,286 (865 fg, 556 ft) in 1967-69
Widest scoring margin in single season:
   10.9 - Maravich, 44.2; Mount, 33.3 (1968-69)
Maravich has also recorded the third highest single game point total in NCAA history:
   69 points (26 fg, 17 ft) vs. Alabama (2-7-70)

SEC RECORDS HELD BY PETE MARAVICH

SINGLE GAME (Conference Only)
Points scored:
   69 (26 fg, 17 ft) vs. Alabama (2-7-70)
Field goal attempts:
   57 (22 made) vs. Vanderbilt (1-29-68)
   57 (26 made) vs. Alabama (2-7-70)
Field goals made:
   26 (54 att.) vs. Vanderbilt (12-11-69)
   26 (57 att.) vs. Alabama (2-7-70)
Free throw attempts:
   27 (22 made) vs. Florida (2-12-69)
Free throws made:
   22 (27 att.) vs. Florida (2-12-69)

SINGLE SEASON (Conference Only)
Points scored:
   851 (336 fg, 179 ft) in 1969-70
Field goal attempts:
   741 (336 made) in 1969-70
Field goals made:
   336 (741 att.) in 1969-70
Free throw attempts:
   243 (199 made) in 1967-68
Free throws made:
   199 (243 att.) in 1967-68

CAREER (Conference Only)
Points scored:
 2,383 (902 fg, 553 ft) in 1967-70
Field goal attempts:
 2,108 (902 made) in 1967-70
Field goals made:
 902 (2,108 att.) in 1967-70
Free throw attempts:
 720 (553 made) in 1967-70
Free throws made:
 553 (720 att.) in 1967-70
Assists:
 257 in 1967-70

SINGLE GAME (Non-conference)
Points scored:
 66 (25 fg, 16 ft) vs. Tulane (2-10-69)
Field goal attempts:
 51 (25 made) vs. Tulane (2-10-69)
Field goals made:
 25 (51 att.) vs. Tulane (2-10-69)
Free throw attempts:
 31 (30 made) vs. Oregon State (12-22-69)
Free throws made:
 30 (31 att.) vs. Oregon State (12-22-69)

SINGLE SEASON (All Games)
Points scored:
 1,381 (522 fg, 337 ft) in 1969-70
Average points per game:
 44.5 (1,381 pts. in 31 gms.) in 1969-70
Field goal attempts:
 1,168 (522 made) in 1969-70
Field goals made:
 522 (1,168 att.) in 1969-70
Free throw attempts:
 436 (337 made) in 1969-70
Free throws made:
 337 (436 att.) in 1969-70
Assists:
 192 in 1969-70

CAREER (All Games)
Points scored:
 3,667 (1,387 fg, 893 ft) in 1967-70
Average points per game:
 44.2 (3,667 pts. in 83 gms.) in 1967-70
Field goal attempts:
 3,166 (1,387 made) in 1967-70
Field goals made:
 1,387 (3,166 att.) in 1967-70
Free throw attempts:
 1,152 (893 made) in 1967-70
Free throws made:
 893 (1,152 att.) in 1967-70
Assists:
 425 in 1967-70

LSU SCHOOL RECORDS HELD BY PETE MARAVICH

SCORING
Points:
 Game: 69 (26 fg, 17 ft) vs. Alabama, 2-7-70
 Season: 1,381 (522 fg, 337 ft) in 1969-70
 Career: 3,667 (1,387 fg, 893 ft) in 1967-70
Average:
 Season: 44.5 (1,381 pts. in 31 gms.) in 1969-70
 Career: 44.2 (3,667 pts. in 83 gms.) in 1969-70

FIELD GOALS
Attempted:
 Game: 57 (22 made) vs. Vanderbilt, 1-29-68
   57 (26 made) vs. Alabama, 2-7-70

Season: 1,168 (522 made) in 1969-70
Career: 3,166 (1,387 made) in 1967-70
Scored:
Game: 26 (54 att.) vs. Vanderbilt, 12-11-69
26 (57 att.) vs. Alabama, 2-7-70
Season: 522 (1,168 att.) in 1969-70
Career: 1,387 (3,166 att.) in 1967-70
Percentage:
Game: .733 (22 of 30) vs. Clemson, 12-20-69
(Based on average of 20 attempts or more per game.)

FREE THROWS
Attempted:
Game: 31 (30 made) vs. Oregon State, 12-22-69
Season: 436 (337 made) in 1969-70
Career: 1,152 (893 made) in 1967-70
Scored:
Game: 30 (31 att.) vs. Oregon State, 12-22-69
Season: 337 (436 att.) in 1969-70
Career: 893 (1,152 att.) in 1967-70
Percentage:
Game: .968 (30 of 31) vs. Oregon State, 12-22-69
(Based on average of 20 attempts or more per game.)

PASSING
Assists:
Season: 192 in 1969-70
Career: 425 in 1967-70
Average:
Season: 6.2 (192 in 31 gms.) in 1969-70
Career: 5.1 (425 in 83 gms.) in 1967-70

PETE MARAVICH NBA CAREER STATISTICS

	YEAR 1970-71	YEAR 1971-72	YEAR 1972-73	YEAR 1973-74	TOTALS
GS	81	66	79	76	302
FGM	738	460	789	819	2806
FGA	1613	1077	1788	1791	6269
PCT.	.457	.427	.441	.457	.448
FTM	404	355	485	469	1713
FTA	505	438	606	568	2117
PCT.	.800	.811	.800	.826	.806
REB	298	256	345	374	1274
AST	355	393	546	396	1690
PTS.	1880	1275	2063	2107	7325
AVG.	23.2	19.3	26.1	27.7	24.2

PLAYOFF STATISTICS

GS	5	6	6		17
FGM	46	54	65		165
FGA	122	121	155		398
PCT.	.377	.446	.419		.414
FTM	18	58	27		103
FTA	26	71	34		131
PCT.	.692	.817	.794		.786
REB	26	32	29		87
AST	24	28	40		92
PTS.	110	166	157		433
AVG.	22.0	27.7	26.2		25.5

ALL STAR GAME STATISTICS

MIN			22	22	44
FGM			4	4	8
FGA			8	15	23
PCT.			.500	.267	.348
FTM			0	7	7
FTA			0	9	9
PCT.			.000	.780	.780
REB			3	3	6
AST			5	4	9
PTS.			8	15	23
AVG.			8	15	11.5